BEAUTIFUL AMERICA

A CUBAN STORY

Dr. Charles Anthony

JONES MEDIA
PUBLISHING

Jones Media Publishing
10645 N. Tatum Blvd. Ste. 200-166
Phoenix, AZ 85028
www.JonesMediaPublishing.com

Printed in the United States of America

ISBN-13: 978-1-945849-78-7 paperback
JMP2019.3

Contents

CHAPTER ONE

Finding Love in Cuba

"Let those who desire a secure homeland conquer it. Let those who do not conquer it live under the whip and in exile, watched over like wild animals, cast from one country to another, concealing the death of their souls with a beggar's smile from the scorn of free men."

-Jose Marti

Enrique leaned against the Harley-Davidson flathead. "Where's your family?"

"Inside buying supplies," America said.

"I've seen you, you know. In the fields."

America gave him a slight grin. "I've seen you too. Well then, why didn't you bring me a lemonade?"

Enrique's smile spread across his face like the morning sun and every tooth appeared like the neon lights shimmering in waves along Avenida de Maceo in Havana. "You know, I've circled the island on my Harley more than once. I also have a sidecar. We could take a ride around town and be back before your family comes out of the store."

"It would ruin my reputation to be seen with you, Enrique."

Enrique smiled again and held back his laughter at the thought of a field hand ruining her reputation with the son of her employer. "Too far below your class, yes?"

It was her turn to smile. "Yes, and besides, I have to get ready for the dance tonight. I have to do my hair and my nails. Then decide what dress to wear."

"The dance in Pinar Del Rio?"

"That exact dance."

He had intended to visit the regular girls in Havana at the local bars this evening, but this girl . . . this girl had spirit, beauty, and there was something captivating in her eyes. He started the Harley. "See you tonight then. What's your name, muchacha? And would you rather ride home in a car or a sidecar?"

"I'd rather walk home with my girlfriends. My name is America." Which is exactly what she did, while Enrique motored along next to them at two miles an hour.

For the next four months he became a frequent visitor in the fields and at night often parked his motorcycle a hundred yards up the road from her house and walked down to the small shack and whistled. America would slip out her window and they would walk in the night enjoying idle conversation and goodnight kisses.

Eventually, that was not enough. She was pregnant within six months of their first meeting. She dreaded having to tell her father. She contemplated various approaches to use when she finally spoke to him. She decided to be ashamed. Then, after he had humiliated her, she said,

"Pipo, you always told me to marry well and to get out of the fields. I didn't plan it this way, but this is what happened."

Her father listened quietly to her explanation. He watched her tears, heard her confession, and was patient as she informed him that Enrique was in love with her and they would marry. She would not be abandoned.

She was surprised when he finally spoke. "No, America, I don't think so. He has too much pride in his Spanish blood. And he's a womanizer. He's also not a Taino. I don't care how much money he has. You are better than this. He has slept with plenty of girls and he'll continue to even after he's married. He flaunts his power and wealth around the island. This man is arrogant and has no manners."

"Pipo, please. He's coming tonight to speak to you about marrying me."

"No, I don't think he'll even show up." He looked into his daughter's eyes. "This man looks down at you, at us." And that was it. With those words, he stood up out of the chair and wandered out to the porch to smoke.

The night proved her father correct. A similar conversation was taking place in the Hacienda of Señor Gomez. "She's beneath you, she's a whore trying to trap you!" yelled Enrique's father. "She's a Taino, her skin's too dark, and she has no link to Spain."

Over the years, America had turned down many men who wanted to court her. She had up until this point been patient and waited for the right man. She thought Enrique was that man. What a fool she had been. All evening America sat on the porch and listened for the sound of the motorcycle, but it never came. He had spoken eloquently about his love, finding words that she marveled at, drawing pictures of poetry to describe the yearning of their hearts. She was certain he loved her, but eventually it all trickled away in a night of tears. There would be no marriage, no escape from the fields, and what remained was only the necessity of an unbreakable heart.

There would be no motorcycle sidecar ride around the island because Enrique Gomez left for Miami as his father demanded. She never saw him again. Their son, Rigoberto Martinez, was born in September 1934.

America gave birth to him at home. She was not allowed to participate in family gatherings. She became an outcast in her parents' eyes and in the community. There was no help from anyone in her family, and America was left alone to find her way as a single mother in Cuba.

Rigo was three when America met Tito Gonzales. There was no courtship. He was fifteen years her senior, a notorious gambler who was celebrating a recent run of good luck. He had won a significant amount of money and two small farms. He was on the third day of his celebration, which had taken him from one cantina to the next.

America was hungry and beautiful. Tito was lonely and drunk. It was an unplanned marriage, but somehow, it worked. America managed the family finances, and the conversations usually went something like this:

"America, where's the money I kept in the cigar box? Where's my gambling money?"

"In the bank, I deposited it today."

"I'm like a slave working on my own farms. You take everything from me and just pay me a wage." He emptied his pockets, and a few meager bills and change spilled onto the table.

"You know the rules, Tito, all the money from the American Fruit Company lease goes into the bank, and I have the savings book right here." She patted her chest. "The other money runs the house, and you can gamble all you want on the wages you make working the farm."

He pointed in the direction of the hidden savings passbook. "You know, a woman's breast can be the coldest thing in the world." And then he would smile and shake his head. She would hand him an extra fifty pesos, he would kiss her and head off into the night. But he was always home when the cantinas closed, his pockets would be mostly empty, but he would snuggle into bed and reach out to kiss his wife.

"Did you win?" she would murmur.

"Now, you know the only thing I've ever really won is your heart, and that's all I need."

Tito treated Rigo well. Rigo took on the last name Gonzalez, though the boy and stepfather never really bonded. There was too much free spiritedness and gentleness in Tito and too much anger, hurt and darkness in Rigo. He inherited his mother's dark Taino features. He accepted and embraced his role as a bastard child. Neither he nor America were wanted by his grandparents, so he grew up with resentment, anger, and a mean temper.

Tito died one week before Rigo's 16th birthday. If America's escape had been to marry well, Rigo's escape would be more suited to his penchant towards violence. The gentle side of his nature, such as taking in stray animals and doctoring them to health, would be hidden in the indoctrination of the La Juventud Militaria (the Military Youth). Supported by the state, young Cubans who had a desire to become soldiers after completing secondary school were indoctrinated into a political agenda that supported the eternal presidency of Fulgencio Batista. For Rigo, this would not be the time for healing and saving others.

The opportunity to find value and meaning in his life presented itself in the form of the Cuban Army. Rigo initially trained as a soldier with the primary purpose of inflicting harm on others. There was however still space in his heart, which yearned for love and healing.

Juanita Maria Martinez was a campesina who worked a fruit farm with her parents. Her life and situation were much like those of America at her age. She was exceptionally bright, and each spring, for three months out of the year, her parents sent her to Old Havana to attend school. Although she wore a traditional Catholic schoolgirl dress, Juanita was lost in the cluster of girls gossiping, talking, and laughing.

They would take lunch in the park, which attracted a variety of young men. Rigo quickly noticed her in the group. The swagger to her step and her clear bright laughter separated her from the others. She was more intent on noticing the crowd than her friends directly in front of her. Her eyes flashed across Rigo and the other soldiers wearing sharply pressed and polished uniforms. Her dress was just a little tighter and shorter than the others. She seemed to want to be noticed, and Rigo obliged.

"Hello, ladies. Look at us strong and handsome men in uniform. Maybe we could have lunch together." Although the soldiers didn't have a lunch and they were headed to the bar. The other men really didn't want to spend time with silly schoolgirls but were more interested in an easy conquest. Rigo looked directly at Juanita.

"If you'll have lunch with us," she said, "we'll all share with you."

They sat under the trees and spread their lunches on the ground. Rigo sat across from her so he could watch her expressions, read her eyes, and attempt to find any level of interest. He was very hungry but purposefully refrained from more than a piece of fruit and half a sandwich. "So where are you girls going to school?"

"La Merced," one of the girls said.

"And what do you study there?"

"Literature, mathematics, and history," Juanita said. "And the nuns teach us how to stay away from boys who ask too many questions."

The girls giggled and Rigo smiled. She had spirit. After finishing lunch he walked them back towards the church and school along La Calle Principal. He stayed close to her all the way back to the school. "Would you come again for lunch in the park?"

"All the girls have to stay together in the city. The nuns won't let us walk alone."

"Of course, bring your friends. I'll bring some of mine from my unit." Rigo wondered whom he could persuade to spend time with schoolgirls.

They were married in the fall. She was sixteen, he a nineteen-year-old soldier in the Cuban Army. It was 1954, four years from disaster.

CHAPTER TWO

Rigo and Tony-
Cuba Libre!

There was something liberating about having a form of transportation. It created freedom and independence. This was true whether it was your first bicycle that allowed you to venture to the next block or a car to the next village. But a new 1953 Harley-Davidson Panhead motorcycle on the island of Cuba was liberation at its finest! Memories involving our vehicles often race across our minds, sometimes for no reason except that they were there when we needed them. With them came moments of joy, regardless of the difficulties life often brought.

Rigo's happiness was derived from his Panhead and the looks it brought from the young ladies walking down Havana's Malecon. The sense of power over the road and riding past his friends gave him moments of indefinable exhilaration. America told Rigo she first met his father while he was riding around the island on just such a motorcycle and so she rewarded her son with the machine once he turned 18 and completed his secondary studies. This bike was smaller than the one his father rode, but still, a Harley nonetheless. She told him the same thing his father Enrique had told her when they first met. "You don't have to go fast. It's a Harley-Davidson. You're already cool."

So, like his father before him, he decided to circumnavigate the island. If his father, whom he never met, could do it, he could do it as well. It would take three days to complete the ride. Pinal Del Rio to Havana, then down to the Southern tip of the island would take a day and a half. The ride back home to Pinal Del Rio would take the same amount of time unless distracted by the beauty of the area and warmth of the Cuban people in the South. He had already settled on his first stop, Havana, to see his cousin Tony.

Tony Prieto was a wild young man and Rigo's idol growing up. He had a way with people and especially the loose young women of Havana. He infrequently worked in the sugarcane fields when out of money, but he hated it. He was a boxer in the barrio in the evening and somewhat of a local hero. Tony had the chiseled physique of an athlete, and his sinful smile was captivating. He was recognized for two things, an easy way with women and an ability to take a punch. A succession of blows always more violent followed if anyone dared to engage Tony physically. Sometimes Tony would take a punch on purpose as this only boosted his anger and heightened his determination to inflict pain on his opponent. He had a short, quickly lit fuse and would not hesitate to knock someone into the dirt who disagreed with him or disrespected his family. He also loved to gamble. He grew up looking for the adrenaline rush and nightlife of the Havana casinos. He was often "escorted" out after a loss or scuffle with the pit boss or another gambler.

Rigo drove to the outskirts of Havana and enjoyed the looks he was getting from the local girls as he cruised down the streets. He pulled up in front of Tony's shabby bungalow and slowly got off the bike. He was getting glares from the neighbors as he dismounted. He gently dropped the kickstand and leaned the bike to the left. This process always ended with Rigo walking away but still looking back at the bike, both to ensure it was firmly supported by the kickstand and to admire his new transportation and freedom.

He never knew what to expect when he visited Tony. Sometimes he would find the good-looking twenty-two-year-old with a swollen face, drunk, or sleeping in the yard. Today proved different. As he reached the door, Rigo heard the not-so-muted sound of a girl screaming and Tony yelling. "Mas rapido, mas rapido!" was the mantra Tony repeated over and over, and the feminine voice was making only sounds, caused by either pain or pleasure. Rigo waited until the noise quieted and the silence again gathered on the street. He waited a moment longer until he heard a match strike followed by a controlled exhale. Rigo gathered his nerve and knocked on the door.

The male voice from inside said, "Quien es?"

"Soy yo, Tony, tu primo Rigo."

"Oye, maricon! Espere te un minuto (hey, you little fag, wait a minute)." He could hear Tony rustling around and then walking to the door. The female voice muttered softly.

Tony opened the door wrapped in a stained bedsheet apparently held up only by his fading erection. The top part of the bedsheet was flung around his shoulder like a Roman Emperor who had just conquered all of Western Europe. Tony had the air of Caesar himself, if not for the cigarette pierced against his lips and the barrage of Spanish curse words coming from his mouth. "Mi Putica (my little bitch)! What are you doing here?"

"Hey, Tony. It's my birthday today, I'm eighteen. I wanted to see you before I take off on my bike ride around the island. After that, I'll be heading out to complete my military training."

"Come mierda (Shit eater)! You're eighteen? You just got some fuzzy little hair on your ass a few weeks ago and now you're eighteen? Why the fuck are you riding a bicycle and going off to the military?"

"Not a bicycle, Tony. I just got a Harley for my birthday."

"Well shit, primo, we gotta celebrate! Come in. Let me get some clothes on and we'll head into town and make us some money and kick some ass. Hell, Rigo, we may even find a little chica afterward to send you off Havana style." He threw his arm around his young cousin. "Since the only hole you'll be seeing for a while will be when you clean your rifle or your buddy bends over in the shower. Come in, soldier boy."

The girl, naked, a trickle of blood by her lip, clung to the bedpost. Tony threw her the bedsheet. "Cover your little ass up." He then marched to the bathroom.

Rigo could hear the splash of urine in the toilet. He glanced at the girl. "Hola, mi nombre es Rigo, que es su nombre?"

Tony poked his head out the bathroom door. "Hey, primo, it's no use. She don't speak Spanish or English. She's Russian. Fucks like crazy but only speaks that Russian shit. Sounds like she's constipated and trying to spit out a booger trapped in her nose. Met her at a club last night and have been banging since two in the morning. I think she's from a town called Moco. Weird, eh? Why would the Russians name a town the same as our word for booger? They got some fucking strange words in that language." He laughed.

"Maybe she was trying to say Moscow, it's their capital."

The young girl pointed to her chest. "Moscow, si." She pointed at Rigo. "Havana, si."

Tony emerged from the bathroom. "Yeah, well, wherever she's from, her ass must go now. Hey, little booger girl, take your panties and young Russian ass and get the hell out of here. I got to entertain my cousin Rigo today. Glad you're not from booger-town." Smiling at Rigo, he threw the girl's pants onto the bed and pointed to the door. The girl grabbed her clothes and stomped to the bathroom.

Tony chuckled. "Goddamn Russians are starting to show up all over the island. Pretty soon they'll have us using vodka in our Cuba libres instead of rum. I don't mind fucking them, but sure as shit I don't trust those bastards. Let's go, my little hombre. I'll show you what real men do when they celebrate in my Havana." The Russian girl emerged from the bathroom and Tony hustled her out the door with a piercing kiss and strong grab on her left ass cheek. They all walked outside and silently admired the Harley.

"Well, primo, what do think?" Rigo asked.

Tony nodded admiringly. "I think it's an American motorcycle. Nice, man, fucking nice."

Rigo smiled. "Let's take a ride around the neighborhood."

"You ain't giving me a fucking ride on that piece of shit. I'm never going to ride with you anywhere."

"I thought you said it was a nice bike."

"Yeah, nice, but no way am I going to ride behind you with your ass rubbing my dick. It's just too weird. If my dick forgets you're a dude, it will fuck my head up for a long time. And I don't need that shit happening to me. As for you riding behind me, nunca, bro, not happening, never."

"All right, Tony. I certainly don't want to mess up your head beyond what it already is, especially the one between your legs."

Tony half smiled and punched him in the arm with a quick jab. The blow knocked Rigo off-balance and he stumbled back. Tony shook his head. "Damn, primo, make sure you get smart in school or stay in the Army. Never rely on your fists, I touched you and nearly broke your arm. All right, man, we'll take my truck. It hurts less when we get drunk and hit a wall. Plus I got to drop the Russian off where I found her. She'll never figure out how to get out of this neighborhood, and when we come back she'll still be sitting on the front porch." He looked around at the neighbors. "What!" They all turned back to their yard work. "I'll put this chica in the truck and follow you back to your farm, we'll drop off the bike and then head into Havana."

America wasn't home, which was a good thing. She didn't like Tony. She said he was trouble and a bad influence on Rigo. They slid the Harley into the shed and finally the 1949 faded-blue Chevy pickup bounced off into the night. The Russian girl rode in the truck bed like she was on a roller coaster until the moment they arrived at the popular Inglaterra Hotel. Tony slammed on the brakes. The girl thumped against the back of the cab, jumped out of the truck bed, smoothed down her skirt, mouthed a stream of what they could only imagine were Russian curse words, and stomped off.

Tony was driving over 60 miles an hour when he slammed on the brakes and pulled up in front of the Montmartre Club. It was centrally located in the Vedado section of Havana. It had long been the only club and casino in Havana that was entirely indoors. The Malecon and Nacional Hotel were only two blocks away and illuminated the backdrop of the bustling city. The interior of the club was designed in a modern style with ornate sculptures and contemporary art. It still had a good reputation and was frequented regularly by locals and tourists alike.

The club was for serious gamblers, and potential trouble lingered in the recesses of Rigo's mind as soon as Tony told him where he was taking them. It was said that Meyer Lansky, the American businessman with connections to the mob, had taken over operation of the club. Rigo glanced at Tony, who was thoughtfully fondling the naked Cuban bobble doll dancing on the truck's dashboard. "Hey, Tony, you sure we want to go here? This is for real money, and I don't want to lose what little I have."

"Spoken like a true little maricon. I didn't ask you for money, little rich boy. I'll take some gringo cash and then we can go find some young putas and good rum. One hour here and then we'll go to the Hotel Nacional. Maybe we'll see some other Russian chicas who want a taste of some good Cuban maduros. Let's go, birthday boy."

As they headed to the casino on the third floor, Tony counted his money. "A hundred pesos. I got to win tonight or I'll have to box again sooner than I really want to. That last guy was fifty pounds heavier than me. He rocked me a couple of times, but then I pounded his kidneys. Too bad for him that he lowered his hands and I broke his jaw. It was real pretty. No cane fields for me. I'd rather take a beating in the ring than work that shit."

Adrenaline pumping, they reached the casino on the third floor and entered the hall. Tony bounced in with much swagger, while Rigo tried to feel comfortable but still walked in his cousin's shadow. They made their way towards a blackjack table with four other Cuban men already playing. A pit boss lounged off to one side and a hostess appeared as soon as they sat down. "Bring us some Cuba libres," Tony said.

The hostess looked nervously at the pit boss. This wasn't a usual order in a Batista-sponsored hotel. The pit boss nodded and she scurried away to fetch their drinks. Rigo glanced around the room, absorbed the atmosphere, and grew apprehensive. Should he follow his cousin's lead and put some of his money on the table? But nothing ventured, nothing lost. He put his meager pesos back in his pocket. This was money for his trip around the island.

"All right, putas, vamonos. Let's win some fucking gringo money tonight." The men at the table cheered and clapped. A blend of smells permeated the casino. Cuban cigars, cheap perfume, sweat, and finally danger mixed to create an aroma of tension. The smoke rose to the ceiling as testosterone spiked in Tony and the other men.

After an hour, Tony had $800 in chips staring back at him. He also had emptied seven glasses of strongly poured rum and Coke. "Hey, Tony, the hour is up, you pounded these gringos. Let's get out of here and head to the hotel. I want to bet on some pretty girls."

"Don't be in such a hurry to crawl back under mommy's skirt. I'm fucking destroying these pigs. These little American gangster boys won't miss the few pesos I win tonight." Tony leaned forward on his chair and raised his voice. "These gringos and their dictator whore have taken plenty from our country!" The pit boss stared at him. Silence echoed. Rigo had been in these situations with his cousin before and knew better than to try to restrain Tony from being Tony.

The pit boss edged his way through the resuming conga beat to where Tony swayed to the music and rum, his finger moving through the smoky air like a swing band conductor's. The pit boss whispered into his ear. "Señor, I must ask you to leave after this drink. You may choose to play at most three more hands, if you wish, then you must go."

Tony leaned to the side like a dog that has just heard an interesting or familiar sound. "What the fuck you mean I'm pretty? I'll slap you across your face until you cry like a little girl. Move away before I pull my zipper down and start slapping." The gamblers at the table broke out laughing.

The pit boss slowly walked away, the hostess smirked, and Rigo buried his head in his hands.

Tony slapped down three bets in a row…and lost them all. His invincible demeanor morphed into anger. Rigo grabbed his arm. "Vamonos, Tony. You had a good night, but it's over, now it's time to go."

"Estos maricones. They tell me to bet so they can take the money." Tony had started slurring his words. "I won! I'll get my money back even if I have to beat it out of these selfish, greedy fucks." He turned to the dealer. "You took all of my money, you prick."

The dealer waved for security. The other men collected their chips from the table. The atmosphere turned threatening. It was too late to rethink his decision to spend his birthday with Tony. Now the task was to get his cousin out of there before they both ended up in jail or in the alley beaten and bloodied.

"Tony, it's my goddamn birthday. Don't fuck it up. Let's get out of here before we get thrown out. Let's leave in one piece before leaving is no longer an option."

For a moment the scales were balanced. Finally, Tony slowly smiled and winked. "Alright, primo. I forgot you're not a fighter. Let's go hunting for some little chicas, and I'll settle this matter later." They stumbled down the marble stairs. Tony smiled and waved at two men heading into the gambling hall. "Be sure to keep one hand on your wallets and one on your balls, my friends, as you may not be able to find either when you leave. The gringo bastards always find a way to take them both away from the men of the island. They'll fuck you just like they continue to fuck our Cuba."

They sat in the truck for a few minutes after Tony slammed the door shut and searched the Havana radio stations. He landed on the popular Tito Puente mambo tune "El Rey del Timbal / Que lindo el Mambo." He grinded the transmission into first gear. "Let's go pussy hunting." The blue truck seemed darker now as the crescent moon gleamed on its hood and it spun out of the parking lot. "Relax, primo, the night is still young."

The circular entranceway to the Nacional Hotel ascended the hill, and the truck sped up the incline and screeched to a stop a few meters from the entrance. Tony reached across Rigo and opened his door. "Get out, primo."

"Why aren't you parking?"

"Of course I'm fucking parking, comedor de mierda! I was doing you a favor by dropping you at the door so that you don't have to walk and stress your little feet on your birthday. Have a drink waiting for me. See you in a few minutes."

Rigo hesitantly stepped out. The door shut behind him as soon as his feet hit the pavement. The truck sped back down the hill headed into either the parking lot or the Havana night. There was no sense in walking after him. He hoped his cousin wouldn't strand him in Havana, again.

Rigo turned to the stairs leading up to the entrance of the sexy building that embraced the Latin rhythms and opulence of the era. He walked past rows of palm trees and entered the archway leading to the hotel lobby. Several Cuban men were toting luggage through the lobby. Older Cubans along the dancehall entranceway were rolling fresh cigars. Guests were busy checking in as Rigo made his way to the Compay Segundo Hall, where the music of El Benny and his Banda Gigante filled the courtyard. Visible from the patio was the ocean's edge, where the sand resembled gold dust sparkling against the caress of the moon and washed clean by the warm waters of the Caribbean. The music rolled along every corridor of the hotel and incited both young and old to sway their hips to the Latin beat. Salsa beckoned like a siren song to anyone looking for a night of liberation and romance.

He headed straight for the bar and again opted for a Cuba libre. At the end of the bar stood the Russian girl. Her blond shoulder-length hair appeared silky smooth against the long red dress. She looked stunning in the evening light. She had three other tempting blond girls huddled up gossiping amongst themselves next to her. From across the bar their faces appeared to glow. He contemplated walking over and starting a conversation but instead reached for some liquid courage. He downed the contents of the glass, almost choking on the lime. He looked at the bartender. "Uno mas, hermano."

The second was much smoother than the first and lacked the taste of rum, although he saw the bartender fill the glass halfway with Bacardi. The liquid warmed his stomach and amplified his courage. Images of the Russian's figure revealed to him earlier danced in his head. His heartbeat accelerated with a level of testosterone only reached in the body of an 18-year-old. He attempted to look uninterested and walked over. "Hola, ladies de Moscow. Which one of you would like to dance?"

The girls were giggling and glancing at each other. Rigo downed the last bit of liquor from his glass, grabbed hold of one girl's hand, and headed for the dance floor. She looked back at the other three girls and smiled. They danced until their shirt and blouse gleamed with sweat. "It's my birthday. Will you help me celebrate tonight?"

Rigo was greeted with a bewildered gaze. There was no way she understood what he suggested. She didn't speak his language, but she understood his hands on her body. Prompted by the pulsating rhythms, he pulled her close to him, and they kissed passionately on the edge of the dance floor for several minutes. He could feel her heat as he shifted his swelling erection closer to her. Already holding her tightly, there was no room for further closeness other than penetration. Suddenly breaking the spell, there was a tap on his shoulder.

It was the girl from Tony's. "Tony?"

Tony had been gone much too long to be only parking the truck. "Si, Tony." Rigo left his new Russian friends and walked towards the hotel exit.

From the top step of the hotel entrance, he could see the blue Chevy in the parking lot. "Tony, have you passed out, drank too much already?" He walked towards the vehicle. No one was in the truck so he explored to the edge of the parking lot. He then saw a figure in the distance. Tony was staggering across the lot. About a hundred yards away from him were four men in a full sprint pursuit. "Shit!" Rigo started running towards the men. Tony stopped and turned around to face the approaching men.

One was the paunchy pit boss from the casino. Tony lunged at the four of them, making contact with the closest one first. He cursed with every blow; his fists exploded in their faces rhythmically. Three men hit the ground. The fourth man backed away a few steps and reached into his coat jacket. At that moment Tony seemed to stand up taller and pumped his chest out at the man, almost daring him to make a move.

Rigo saw the flashes before he heard the echo of the exploding bullets. With the first shot, Tony charged the man wielding the gun. The second shot jerked his left shoulder back and brought him to the ground before he reached the man. There were five shots in all. Each one found its way into Tony, who now lay on his back in the gravel.

The smoke cleared, but the acrid sulfur smell would forever be burned into Rigo's memory. He was just feet away from Tony when the man pointed the pistol at him and signaled him to stop. The four men limped away from the body and headed back in the direction of the gambling hall. They glanced back every few steps to ensure no one followed them. Rigo began to run towards the men then stopped and looked back at Tony. The pool of dark blood continued to expand, creating a silhouette that grew with every passing second. "Primo! Qué has hecho? What have you done?"

Blood seeped from Tony's mouth. "I...won, Rigo." He moved his right hand slightly and pointed towards his pocket. Rigo reached in and took out $800 American dollars. "I won...I won." Tony held a slight smile for a short time and then began to cough. Blood trickled from the corner of his mouth.

"Yes, Tony, you won, my cousin, you always win." Rigo cried. There was nothing else for him to do but hold Tony close and allow his soul to be set free. Other people strolled through the parking lot whispering and pointing but did not offer help. They simply looked, assumed, and judged. Soon they would forget their brief and insignificant encounter amid a night of dancing and drinking, only slightly inconvenienced by the murder of a fellow Cuban. So was the character of Havana. Such would be the fate of the island.

CHAPTER THREE

A Soldier is Born

It was all inside Rigo. Periodically, he mustered some interest in life to be civil around others or lost himself in rum long enough to enjoy a night out with his friends. However, Tony's death, the lingering humiliation of being a bastard, and his mother's apparent neglect had burrowed into him and he struggled to find meaning in his life. The motorcycle sat abandoned in the shed except when he dared fate and roared down the highway with the engine screaming, clawing for speed beyond its capacity. His demeanor had become darker, and the village girls who had opened to him like a flower now made excuses not to be seen with him. Even his best friends said he was difficult to be around. It was this gloomy period in his life that haunted Rigo and guided him from the age of innocence to manhood. One of his friends commented to another, "He has become more like Tony than Rigo." He needed direction. It was time he learned a skill more in line with his new state of mind. He would learn to be a soldier.

At eighteen years of age but with a lifetime of experiences and loss, Rigo stepped off the recruit bus in Bayamo Cuba and into a barrage of profanity and panic. Together with the other young men, he was herded into a line and screamed at by several Cuban soldiers. As his first foot hit the ground stepping off the bus, his scanning gaze glimpsed a blond and soulfully blue-eyed American. This man was confident, casual, and obviously in a position of authority. Next to him the familiar and unfriendly face of Jose Rojas. Now a lieutenant, Rojas glared at him behind the end of the half-smoked cigarette affixed to his bottom lip. Rojas was three years older and from one of the poorer families in Pinar Del Rio. His family had worked on one of America and Tito's farms for a few years. He resented the land and money that came from gambling. He detested the fate that many Cubans fell victim to in the casinos and backroom parlors of Havana. He especially resented the acquisition of land from families who lost all their money and dignity to this terrible vice. To Rojas, Rigo was a pawn of the American-owned fruit companies. Rojas was still bitter over a drunken run-in he'd had at a community party that resulted in a fight in which 16-year-old Rigo had broken his nose. Rojas moved through the ranks until he came to a halt a few centimeters from Rigo's face.

"Well, what have we here? My old friend Rigo. I didn't recognize you without a drink in your hand or a puta on your lap. I can still hear the many foul words you so easily screamed at your cane workers to keep them in line. Why are you here, rich boy? Surely you don't think you can become a soldier. You need to be truly strong to finish this training. And you can't gamble, drink, or punch your way through this place. You need discipline, which comes with hard work and patience. You, little man, need to return to the bus and head back to the farm and the local bar you crawled out of. I'm sure your mother has a nice soft spot waiting for you in Pinar Del Rio."

But this was not Pinar Del Rio. Rigo slowly unclenched his fists, chose a spot to stare at just above the lieutenant's cap in the distance. "Sir! I will complete the training for my country and family." By this time, all eyes were on the pair. The American still lounged against the wall in an easy stance, but he too seemed interested in the confrontation. This must be more than just the regular harassment of the recruits.

"Your family? Oh, you mean your mother America and the other whores, the other abusers of the people, the thieves of Cuba? Let me ask you, boy, do you pay the whores in money you steal from the backs of your workers, or win it by cheating in card games like the rest of your family? I guess that's a question I could ask your father. But wait…he's somewhat of a mystery, isn't he? That's right, Rigo, you're a bastard aren't you?"

At that moment, the American, known as El Rubio, must have sensed the moment had passed from harassment to challenge and might erupt into a fight, which would not do well for discipline among the other recruits. He called the group to attention. His Spanish was filtered through an American southern drawl.

"Calmate, soldado. If you want to be a soldier you'll need to be tougher than a dumb-ass reaction to a superior officer. If you want to make it out of here as a soldier, you must become hardened to words and deeds. If we get into your head during training, the enemy will be able to when it really matters and lives are at stake. Don't react too hastily. Learn to assess your situation and make life-saving decisions. Not just for yourself but for the men in your unit." His eyes again came to rest on Rigo after scanning all of the recruits. "Who are you, and what do you want here?"

"Rigoberto Gonzalez. I'm here to serve my country. Whatever conditions you believe will serve me, sir, I'm willing to take harsh words and discomfort. I want to be a soldier. I'm a Cuban patriot."

"Lieutenant Rojas seems unconvinced of your patriotism." El Rubio glanced at Rojas, who was still seething, then returned his eyes to Rigo. "But we shall see." He nodded to Rojas, who took his position in front of the ranks. He called the platoon sergeant forward, they saluted, and the sergeant wheeled to face the men and began barking orders with a raspy voice.

"Let's go, my new little patriots. Let's see how tough your determination can be when pain and suffering become your reward for loyalty. Leave everything here. We'll get your uniforms, boots, and gear later. For now, grab a rucksack from the pile and come with me. You'll find heavy stones to fill them up and then we go running, Cuban soldier style, held down by the weight of the very earth you claim to protect. And look." He pointed at the gathering clouds. "We'll have good weather, some rain to train! What could be better, amigos, than Cuban rain on our heads, Cuban rocks on our backs, and the Cuban earth at our feet?" The sergeant had a huge grin on his face.

Three weeks into training, Rigo had lost twenty pounds. Lieutenant Rojas had made sure he received extra attention. This included mess hall duty, latrine duty, guard duty, and extra physical training every day and evening. Rojas had intended it to break him, but the hardships had only fortified his tenacity and made him stronger.

El Rubio had remained reserved and observed from a distance, huddled with the instructors, assessing the men. He had been taking notes after each training session. At the beginning of the second week of training he had individually interviewed all the men and had asked Rigo what he wanted to do after the military. Rigo explained he wanted to help people suffering and perhaps work in medicine. El Rubio had only nodded and made notes in his book, never helping Rigo, but never making it more difficult either. The word on the base was that he was an American Army training expert helping ensure the Cuban army was maintaining high standards in preparing soldiers who would eventually see combat in support of the democracy. He also helped determine what specialty the soldiers would be assigned to after basic training.

On this particular day, all thoughts of life beyond training, such as family, medical school, and relationships, would disappear into the jungles of Cuba. The sergeant growled at the recruits. "All right, putas, you're going on a little pleasure trip. We'll see who'll survive this training. Many of you won't make it."

Each man was assigned a partner, Rigo briefly glanced at his. The choice was purposeful. Juan Dominica Peña was a seemingly insignificant soldier not just short in stature but also scrawny. His family worked on a horse ranch in the southern part of the island in the town of Bayamo where the training camp was located. Rigo liked Juan. He was simple in attitude, a boy who wanted to do his part although he didn't have much to offer physically. He was highly motivated and always gave his best effort regardless of the task. The instructors didn't respect him. His lack of physical prowess put him at the back of the pack during exercises and training. He was the runt of the litter. He lagged during long-distance runs and would struggle to keep up on every march. His rucksack appeared to be as large as he was, and it took all his strength and effort to finish every training exercise. Neither the taunts from the instructors nor the harsh conditions kept Juan from appearing upbeat and charging forward.

Rigo admired his attitude and respected him. He had offered on a few occasions to help by carrying some of the rocks from Juan's sack. Juan would always say, "Gracias, amigo, pero este es mi cruz (this is my cross to bear)." Rojas had made this pairing so that Rigo would be slowed down in whatever this exercise was.

"Shut up!" Rojas screamed at the silent men. "You will be dropped off in the middle of the night unaware of your location and surroundings. You will have no food. You are expected to make it to your final checkpoint within seventy-two hours. There will be a flag representing our unit that you must secure without getting caught by the opposing forces. The OPFOR will be made up of instructors and camp leaders. The first team to reach the flag will get a two-day pass. I don't recall anyone actually ever getting to the flag, but you niñas need something to strive for."

Rojas gave them a vicious grin and threw a pile of blindfolds on the ground. "I forgot to tell you about these. Put one on and do not take it off until we drop you off." They all did so. "If you peek under your blindfold, you won't like the kick in the ass you'll get for being a cheater. You won't always have a partner in combat, but when you do you must take care of each other. You must both make it to the extrication point for you to pass. You'll each have a whistle that should only be used if you're hurt, dead, or it's after the third day at 11:59 pm. If any of you girls whistle because your tummy hurts or you broke a nail, I'll make your life here at our private resort a living hell. You all have everything you need to survive: a knife, a whistle, a partner, survival instincts, and your own will. You have all seen the maps and hopefully will be able to coordinate your knowledge of the terrain and the map to your memory and know in which general direction your extraction point will be. Get your asses on the truck."

Rigo and Juan jumped on the back of the truck with the blindfolds wrapped securely over their heads. They sat quietly, each to his own predetermined task they'd hurriedly discussed. Juan kept track of the turns in the truck, plotting the direction. Rigo tried to judge the speed of the truck and the distance they traveled. They each had memorized portions of the map. An hour later the first team was dropped off, and then another team every half hour. The instructors yelled, "Salga de aquí (Get out of here)!"

Another hour passed, and the truck stopped. This time there was no yelling, simply the sound of the truck tailgate lowering followed by a sharp pain of a military boot on Rigo's back. He hit the ground hard on his side and bounced on hard gravel. Another thump was followed by laughter. By the time Rigo peeled off his blindfold, searching for light, the truck was out of sight and down the road.

"Hijo de puta! I should have expected that. You okay, Juan?"

"One of the benefits of being little. I weigh less and am closer to the ground."

It was pitch black. "Do you remember the bridge we ran across during our long runs?" Rigo said. "Made of wood with long steel girders on both sides? Long and very high over the river?"

"I slipped on the steel and busted my ass during our last run."

"Somewhere back there about twenty-five minutes or so ago we crossed something that sounded like that bridge."

"I think so too." He pointed to the sky. "Look, the North Star."

"I think we went in circles a couple of times. Even subtracting the cutbacks, if that was the bridge, then we're about 20 kilometers from the base, which would mean we're in zone A6 of the map." Rigo turned to face Juan. "Remember the checkpoint in A6?"

"The length seemed correct. If that was the bridge, we made four right turns. At least that's how I saw it in my mind. I'm sure they were trying to confuse us. Maybe the extraction point is just getting back to the damn base. If we're wrong, then we're in a world of shit. We might just walk off the island and into the ocean. If we head east and skirt the creek, we can possibly run right along the south entrance of our basecamp. Lead the way, jefe."

Rigo shook his head. "We're equals out here, I'm no one's boss. We have a couple of hours of night left before the pricks come looking for us, but let's get off the road. I wouldn't put it past them to drop us off and then have an ambush waiting for us just up the road. They said the first team to make it in past the OPFOR gets a two-day pass. I could use getting into a bit of trouble and having some fun in Havana before we go back to getting our asses kicked."

"I'd love to get home and see my little boy," Juan said almost like a prayer.

Sure enough, a kilometer down the road, they saw the pinpoints of lit cigarettes and heard muted conversation. Rojas had set a trap for them, but it would take more than that to capture them. They eased into a creek bed and meandered through the jungle and around the trap. They traveled slowly and circumvented several attempted ambushes, traveling over 10 kilometers during the first 24 hours.

On the second day of survival training, Juan and Rigo figured they were about nine kilometers from basecamp. They moved at night and slept during the day, hiding under leaves and undetected by the OPFOR, who were only a few feet away from them at times. They fed on the plentiful fruit, which led to many stops to empty their bowels. They were fatigued but hydrated from drinking from the creek and nourished from the abundant wild bounty available in the jungle. Night finally fell, the time for moving, the time to make it to the objective and claim their reward.

Juan made the sign of the crucifix, and they took off. "We should move away from the creek," Rigo said. "They'll be looking for us near water. I already heard whistles going off. Either four teams have been hurt or the instructors are playing head games to confuse us." They continued moving slowly, stopping every twenty meters to listen. Several hours passed, and then around midnight they heard voices coming from the creek. Someone had been found. Minutes passed before they heard another whistle indicating that someone else was hurt or captured. An hour passed before the two men slipped back onto the trail and inched along in a low crawl.

At the precise moment Rigo turned to whisper to Juan, there was a crunching sound on the path ahead and the ping of a grenade handle. Rigo leapt to his left, but Juan was struck by something and tumbled down the creek bed into the water. Instinctively, Rigo hurled himself in the direction of the grenade, scooped it up like a baseball infielder, and hurled it across the creek. Rigo ran toward Juan and draped himself over the small soldier who now lay motionless in the creek.

After several seconds, Rigo realized the eminent explosion was no longer eminent. It was either a dud or training grenade, thrown in their direction to flush them out. There was no time to waste. "Juan, you okay?" Rigo whispered.

Juan was breathing but unconscious. Rigo ran his hands across Juan's limbs and found a bump protruding from his leg. Directly under his knee, the bone was jutting through his skin—a compound fracture. Juan started to come to. "Shit. What the fuck did I do? My leg feels numb. What hit me?"

"It's broken, my friend. It's time to blow the whistle and get you some medical treatment. We almost made it back. You did great, Juan." He patted Juan's back and raised the whistle towards his mouth.

Juan pulled Rigo's arm away. "Hell, no. That's not the way we're going finish this. You want to be a doctor someday? Well, fix me up enough to keep moving."

"Are you crazy, hombre?"

"It's my damn leg. I fucked it up when I fell. Shut up and fix it."

Rigo sighed. "Okay. I'll have to pull your bones back into alignment before I splint it. I won't lie, this is going to hurt like hell. Put this stick between your teeth." He put one foot on Juan's chest and took hold of his foot with both hands. Juan closed his eyes and bit down on the stick. He moaned for a few seconds and then passed out. This let Rigo splint the leg efficiently. He placed two branches opposite each other and secured them at the top and bottom with both of their belts. He removed his undershirt, swaddled it against the point of the break and tied it off above the break.

After a while, Juan drifted back to consciousness. Several minutes passed and neither man spoke. Rigo simply listened to the sounds of the jungle, then stood. "Let's go."

Rigo helped Juan up, and he rested his 130-pound frame on his one good leg and leaned on his partner. They moved towards the camp. Their pace was slow, but they made progress. After a few hours they appeared to be only 100 yards away from the camp entrance. The darkness of the evening was occasionally interrupted by moments of light as they passed areas in the forest where the canopy opened above them revealing the stars. The men stopped and sat behind a large tree catching their breath and contemplating their next move.

"There's no way we can simply walk across the base gate without getting caught," Rigo said. "We need a distraction."

"Your call, Rigo. I'm moving like a pregnant snail."

"I'll be right back." Rigo crawled along the tree line to a position west of the gate. He gathered some small twigs and dried branches, then pulled out their last two matches. The first match started the kindling smoking but it didn't catch fire. With the second and final match, a flame finally appeared. He had picked a spot where the fire, with the creek on one side and a clearing on the other, wouldn't spread beyond the small bush.

He quickly returned to Juan's position. From behind a tree he saw the fire begin to grow. The guards moved from the gate towards the fire and began to blow their whistles. Both guards were in a full sprint running to the west away from where Rigo and Juan were waiting. This was their only opportunity, and they seized the moment. Juan prepared himself for the remaining distance knowing it would be a struggle. Rigo grabbed him and placed him on his back like a rucksack. Juan's arms were wrapped around Rigo's neck and his hand rested on his chest. The two glided through the night as one.

With every step, Juan grunted in pain, but the victory flag was still in place on a makeshift pole just past the camp entrance. With 50 yards left and their energy exhausted, they moved now solely on adrenaline. When they were less than 25 yards from the flag, the guards saw them and started to yell. All the guards ran at a full sprint towards the camp entrance. They closed the gap to fewer than ten feet just as both reached for the flag. Not sure they were going to make it, they both grabbed hold of the flag at the same time.

Rigo gently lowered Juan to the ground and leaned over him as they both held the flag in their hands and shared in the moment. Then Rigo collapsed on the ground next to Juan. They now shared the flag while staring up at a million stars and simply smiled. The guards approached them. They were not alone. Their faces along with El Rubio's blocked out the stars as they came into view directly above the exhausted men.

Lieutenant Rojas yelled, "Ay, Dios mio! Anybody but these two! How in God's name did you pull this shit off?"

Juan looked up and whispered, "He is my God too. Like it or not, amigos, we are the champions." Out of the corner of his eye, Rigo caught sight of El Rubio's smile.

CHAPTER FOUR

The Road to Santiago de Cuba

Rigo completed his advanced training and was commissioned as a lieutenant and medic in the Cuban Army. There were times when he simply wanted to return home and live out his days running the farms with his family. He understood, however, that there would be no farms and no freedom as he knew it if Castro was able to win over the Cuban people and the island itself. There was no doubt in the minds of soldiers and civilians alike that he would punish all who served against him.

The sticky, almost palpable air was difficult to take in. With each inhale the thick humidity stuck to the back of your throat and breathing became more like panting. As you swallowed you could feel and taste the warm, musty air. Sweat glued clothing to your body. The salt created by hours of perspiration left men clawing at their backs for relief from the constant itching. You could vividly see the heat rising from the trees in undulating waves.

The south-central town of Camaguey was a good respite and safe haven for the muchachos of the Eighteenth Battalion, supporters of El Presidente Batista. Some soldiers were present when Castro attempted his ill-fated assault in 1953 on the Moncada Barracks in Santiago. The locals would never forget the nineteen dead soldiers of the Eighteenth Battalion. The town treated them with respect and they had no major incidents during the two weeks they spent regrouping and planning for offensive operations. In 1958, the rebels wouldn't dare attack a city that showed allegiance for El Presidente. Instead they remained in areas that had many peasants and farmers, believed to be supporters of their cause. From there they launched isolated guerilla attacks in the remote villages where they could provoke the poor to hope for a more equitable, free Cuba. Unfortunately for Batista and his military men, this was becoming an easier task as the country was seeing little benefit from an ongoing relationship with the "puppet" president of the Americanos.

The average Cuban was poor, relied mostly on farming, and traded for supplies that couldn't be grown on their farms. The peasants worked in the fields and rarely visited Havana with all her lights and glamor. Many of these were macheteros, sugarcane cutters, seasonally employed four months out of the year and more acquainted with hunger and hard work than the opulence of the inner circle of Havana. These men and women served as the backbone upon which the ruling elite built their fortunes.

Havana was well known as a tourist destination but primarily for Americans taking a short trip from the east coast of Florida looking for some "Latin spice." The Havana mob was an assorted mix of characters and underworld figures who owned the night. Pleasure seekers and desperate souls searched Havana for an escape and opportunities to realize forbidden fantasies. People such as Charles "Lucky" Luciano,

Meyer Lansky, Santo Trafficante, Albert Anastasia, and other gangsters had more influence on the island than elected officials and in some cases Batista himself. They were making millions off casinos, drug trafficking, and prostitution. Places like the famous Copacabana Club pulsing on the Malecon in Havana Vieja were packed every night with these Americanos. These were mostly scheming men looking for the local flavor of a tropical interlude with all things sinful, intoxicating, and wrapped in the caress of an exotic Cuban night.

Latin beats echoed throughout the night at many casinos, hotels, and brothels until the sun made its presence known by peeking over the tides of the ocean beaches. With exception of the Cuban elite and girls looking for American opportunities, the average Cuban did not share in the invigorating rhythms and calypso pleasures of Havana. But Havana was far from Camaguey and the men of the Eighteenth Battalion.

The convoy of jeeps left Camaguey headed for Santiago de Cuba intending to help put down rebel activity that recently included an attack on a military outpost. The rebels left with over 100 rifles and a large supply of ammunition. Company C, an infantry unit of 80 men in the Eighteenth Battalion, was given the task of finding and capturing or killing the rebels. The soldiers all understood there was a good chance of getting ambushed en route, but they dutifully accepted the dangers at hand.

As a medic and lieutenant, Rigo was positioned close to the commander in case of an attack. He traditionally traveled in the third jeep of the convoy. The battalion commander had clearly explained the mission to the officers and sergeants, and they knew once they reached the town of San Luis, patrols would be sent out into the jungle to search for the rebels. That is, unless they struck first.

At twenty-three years of age, some considered Rigo "el viejo," an old man. Two weeks previously, Rigo had been surprised when now Captain Jose Rojas arrived and took command of Company C. Rigo hadn't seen him since training camp. Captain Rojas's skepticism about and dislike for Rigo was still very evident to everyone. The thought of their having to rely on each other seemed to make him more cautious in his criticism of Rigo, who, unlike the newly arrived captain, was respected, even loved by all of the men. Rojas seemed to conjure up animosity with his barking commands and disrespectful attitude towards the company. He wanted everyone to know he was in charge. The men were not at all pleased with their new commander, least of all Rigo.

They traveled slowly. The soldiers in the lead jeep remained on guard and alert. In the third jeep, Rigo chatted with Miguel, his eighteen-year-old driver. Miguel described his girlfriend who lived in Matanzas about 50 miles west of Havana. "Of course she'll wait. True, she's the prettiest girl in the village, but that muchacha knows quality. I've been with her for a year now and showed her I'm faithful and hardworking. Besides, in the bedroom, I've given her more pleasure than she'll ever find in this life."

Years ago, when Rigo was Miguel's age, he had thought his own perceived powers as a creator of pleasure were what fashioned a close relationship. Now, at twenty-three, married, with two children, and having experienced so much, he knew better.

"Miguel, your penis isn't a ballistic missile or magic wand. You may be a cock-smith of a rare variety, but don't rely on sex and beauty as the main ingredients of love. Connect your soul to a woman in a lasting way. You think you know women but you don't. You'll make a million mistakes with women and believe the nice things they say mean they love you and will never leave you. You assume they'll put up with your bullshit, but they won't. Most of them are looking for more. Smart girls understand they won't stay young or have perfect bodies forever. They want security, someone who'll stay with them in spite of sometimes being brujas (witches). They'll test your loyalty. If they know you have wandering eyes, they'll watch you and see if you get too close to one of their girlfriends. Here's a suggestion, my friend, look inside her heart and know her joys and fears. But most importantly, Miguel, find a woman who can cook. We all grow old and lose our appetite for sex, but we'll always be hungry."

Miguel nodded slowly. "Okay, I'll do it. I'll fall in love with a fat ugly cook and make her my wife. If I eat and get fat, then she won't be able to see my dick anymore, and sex won't matter." He turned to Rigo. "You're crazy, man. No disrespect, but are you one of those maricones? If you don't like women, then who gives a shit what they look like?"

"Miguel, if you get shot, I may just let you bleed out."

"Okay then, it's settled. I'll marry your sister."

"Since I don't have one, you'll have to marry me."

Both men enjoyed a moment of laughter and connection.

As the sun descended, they reached the mountainous area some seventy miles outside Santiago de Cuba near Bayamo not far from Rigo's old training site. The convoy ground to a halt as a young man who looked like a farmer hobbled up the road towards them waving his arms. The soldiers took their weapons off safety. Captain Rojas stepped out of his jeep. "Que paso, chico?"

The man slowed to a stop. "We were headed back to my brother's farm and my cousin must have fallen asleep. The crash threw me out of the car. I'm okay, just scrapes and bruises, but the car went over the cliff with my cousin inside." He walked to the edge of the road and pointed down. "Please, please can you help my cousin? He's just a kid."

Rojas shrugged. "Sorry, amigo. We're on a mission and there's no road down into the valley."

The young man pointed back the way they'd come. "The road about three kilometers back winds down into the valley. Fifteen minutes at most. Please, sir, won't you help a fellow Cuban?"

Rojas looked impatient. "Sorry, my friend. I hate to say it, but your cousin is probably dead."

"I know it's a long way for the car to fall, but he could still be alive. I'm a farmer, just a simple person asking for help. I beg you."

"We have orders." Rojas turned and started towards his vehicle.

"Is this the way of El Presidente's army? You turn your backs on a Cuban patriot asking for help?"

Rojas whirled around and gave the farmer a hard stare. Meanwhile, the men had started their own conversations, most of the soldiers were out of their jeeps, and they smoked, talked, and peered over the edge of the cliff at the wreckage below.

Miguel yelled, "Captain, the man in the car waved his arm!"

Rigo grabbed his medic pouch, slung the long canvas strap over his head and headed towards the edge of the cliff. "Para el Carajo (the fuck with it)! I'll meet you in a few minutes, Captain. Just keep driving down the road. Miguel can turn around and drive down to where this man mentioned. By the time he arrives, I'll have made an assessment, and if we can save this man, then we will. We'll bring him with us and meet you down the road." He uttered the last words out of the side of his mouth as he took his first step off the cliff and started sliding and bouncing down the side of mountain.

"What the hell are you doing, Lieutenant? You are not to go down to that vehicle!" But Rigo kept going. The last thing he heard Rojas say was, "Leave him here for the rebels to find." The engines started and the convoy moved off.

CHAPTER FIVE

A Leap of Faith

The adrenaline kicked in as Rigo stumbled down the cliff using his buttocks and hands to help slow the speed of descent. He tried to brake his out-of-control plummet by digging his boot heels into the jagged rocks, which minimally reduced the speed of the fall. The rocks were covered with dew, and now some of his own blood apparently seeped from his hands. His attempt to grasp a fixed object only led to sparks of pain and frustration. He questioned the wisdom of his rash reaction, which had only partially been about his desire to help or use his skill as a medic. It was fueled by his dislike of Rojas and the principle that all people in the country should be helped. His duty as a soldier was to serve the people, unlike his commander, who often placed his own self-interest above all else.

He averted the larger rocks by shifting his balance and weight. He'd once again let his emotions guide his actions and ignored the prudence of rational thought. He had to keep his body from flipping headfirst into a boulder or this would be the last decision he regretted. Rojas's leadership was part of a greater problem that plagued Cuba. Everyone saw the problems in the country, but no one did a damn thing about it.

Cuba was no better off today than when the Spaniards enslaved the island. We demonized the rebels as criminals attempting to take over the island, yet others, only 90 miles from our shore, risking nothing, had already done that. We could question the politics and politicians after we got rid of Castro. Or perhaps it was El Presidente who was the problem?

At that moment his thoughts were interrupted as the rocks slipped under his feet at an even greater speed. The last ten meters led him directly toward a boulder at the bottom of the cliff, contact with which left him flat on his back and close to unconsciousness. He drifted back and began doing a mental survey of his limbs. There would be many bruises, but nothing seemed broken or severely cut. He stood, dusted himself off, then made his way to the vehicle only several yards away.

His breath was taken away, not just by the magnitude of the accident, but the car lying upside down near the creek. He hadn't realized from the vantage of the road that the 1953 Buick Skylark was a convertible. Perhaps Miguel had only said he saw a man's hand waving because he knew Rigo wanted to stand up to the Captain. No one could have lived through the plummet down a cliff.

Only the mangled wreckage and a distorted human body were visible. His stomach tightened. There could be no hope for a man in an upside-down convertible. The car itself, every Cuban boy's dream, was a crumpled ruin. The man he came to save surely would have met the same fate.

He got down on his hands and knees and looked inside. A man was wedged between the ground and the floorboards of the car with the back of his head resting against the bottom of the steering wheel. Rigo slid on his belly towards the folded man.

"Oye, muchacho, can you hear me?" Only silence answered. As he'd learned in military school, he reached inside and placed his fingers on the man's neck, found the carotid artery, and pressed firmly. To his surprise, he felt a slight pulse. Could his mind be playing tricks? That was a question only God could answer, not Rigo. He knew he had to remove the man from the car and try to save him. God would intervene when and if he was good and ready.

He quickly jumped to his feet and looked for a way to pull the unconscious man out. Rigo bent over and rested his lower back on the driver's door and the window opening. The window was rolled down which made it easier for him to leverage his weight with his leg strength. He was concerned he would cause more injury if he were not able to pull the man out but saw no better alternative. Pushing up with his legs and straightening his back, he lifted the car a couple of inches and tried to drag the man out by his shirt. By his third attempt he knew it was useless. He cursed the Captain and God's passive indifference.

"Hey there, sir, looks like you need someone stronger than you." Miguel made his way through the underbrush.

"Where'd you come from?"

"Sir, if you'd looked around, you'd have seen the path."

"Miguel, I felt a pulse."

"If he's not dead then he's an alien for sure. Mira, look at him, the guy's purple."

Rigo sniffed. Gasoline was now seeping out of the tank and collecting on the ground. "Shut up and help me get this guy out of the car."

Miguel moved towards the car door and placed his rifle on a boulder. The men resumed Rigo's previous position, but now with twice the strength. On the second try the car moved enough for Miguel to kick a large rock and wedge it underneath the car. Rigo grabbed the man and pulled him out. Now for the first time they saw the face of the young man. He was about the same age as Miguel and reminded Rigo of himself when he was younger. This could have happened to him as he rode his Harley across the island. He felt a sense of responsibility. It was more than coincidence, he owned that moment and believed what he did or didn't do in this instant would not just be the act of a good Samaritan but also define and shape him as a man and soldier. He glanced at Miguel.

"Sir, we can do nothing here, God has spoken."

Rigo knelt and put his ear to the man's chest. By this point it appeared as if their hearts were fused and the beat in his own heart was rhythmically aligned with the man he touched. He removed the farmers shirt, a white guayabera stained in blood. All his training had not prepared him for a moment such as this. Seconds seemed like hours, and the current situation sped by beyond his understanding. He had only practiced lifesaving, but this was real.

With two fingers, Rigo reached back into the area by the tonsils and beyond to ensure the airway was clear of any food or debris. He found the breastplate and placed his thumb in the center. He extended his fingers and used the heel of his hand to identify the correct location on the abdomen. He then began thrusting the palm of one hand covered by the palm of other, his arms locked at the elbow and fully extended. After the third thrust, green-yellow vomit followed by a huge wad of gum shot up into Rigo's face. The projectile fluid mixed with the bright red blood oozed onto Rigo's shirt. He didn't stop, he didn't rest, he simply continued to administer CPR.

Miguel had wondered off a few steps and was bent down gagging as he wiped his own vomit from his face. He prayed that maybe this was the reason the man could not breathe. Rigo placed his head by the man's mouth and listened, then returned to straddling the man and began again. At the thirtieth pump he returned to breathe into his mouth. Miguel watched and counted. Rigo performed this routine over and over;

the humidity soaked him through as if he had jumped into a river with all his clothes on. He seemed to be in a trance.

Over an hour later, Miguel heard the roar of engines in the valley heading north towards them. He was scared to interrupt Rigo, but eventually found his voice. "I think his time has passed, sir. You've done all you could. Let the man go. We should find the rest of our company." Hearing no response, he put his hand on Rigo's shoulder.

"Get your hands off me or this man will die while you stand there in your own fear!" Rigo's eyes seemed far away and appeared to be replaying something from his past. What could give a man such focus of purpose as to completely disregard obvious reality and his own safety?

"Rigo, Lieutenant, we need to move. It may be the rebels." He pointed south towards the noise. "Please, I beg you, let's take the path to the road." The sounds of the vehicle were quickly approaching, but Rigo wouldn't stop. Miguel ran behind a tree as jeeps rolled to a stop a few feet from Rigo and the still body beneath him. A man in civilian clothes jumped out of the first of the two vehicles with a bag in his hands followed by two other soldiers from Company C. They approached the connected men.

Sergeant Flores looked at the situation. "Lieutenant, we brought a doctor. We're to stay with you until picked up by Captain Rojas after he refuels his jeep."

Rigo had taken on the appearance of the town vagabond, covered in filth and sweat like a demon-possessed soul. What he was fighting to save, only God knew.

Perhaps sympathetic to the situation and the young medic's mental state, the village doctor spoke calmly, quietly. "Oye, hermano—listen, brother, it's my turn to help. Let the soldiers put him in the jeep so we can get him back to the clinic. We'll have a better chance of helping him there."

Rigo finally stood up, palms faced forward at his sides as if frozen in place from the persistent thrusting. His gaze didn't leave the body, but he stepped back and let the men lift the man onto the field gurney.

Miguel stepped out onto the road. "Hola muchachos! Am I glad to see you. I was just going up to the road to look for help. As ordered by my lieutenant. Right, Rigo?"

Slowly, as if returning from a long dreamless sleep, Rigo drifted back to the reality of the moment. "Miguel, go with these men and the doctor to the clinic. Stay with this man until his family arrives." Two men placed the body in one of the jeeps and accompanied the doctor in the other.

Both jeeps began to roll. The doctor along with the body was in the second jeep, which inched away slowly. He looked back at the few soldiers that stayed behind with the wreckage. None of the men understood why Rigo couldn't accept the reality of the situation, but the doctor knew. As medical men they knew that hopelessness was a perspective and chose life in the face of death, often reaching for the hidden pulse of God in the midst of darkness. This type of man had difficulty accepting the inevitability of lost hope. Death faced an admirable foe on this day. Rigo would never surrender, no matter what the odds or the degree of danger and hopeless. The men in the jeep discussed the lieutenant and by the time they reached the clinic, they concluded they were lucky to serve with such a dedicated officer and medic. The event would define their relationship and trust. They knew they could always count on him to give them all he had, his very life if needed. Sometimes, how a person deals with the adversity of the moment was the only sign of how they would react in life-threatening situations.

CHAPTER SIX

Until the Sun Also Rises

"A man's troubles are never really overcome until he decides to accept the past for what it is, a book of images that can either serve to strengthen or to weaken. How they serve is a choice made daily and often

-Dr. Charles Anthony

The remainder of the day passed quickly. Lieutenant Rigoberto Gonzalez continued to contemplate its events. Darkness began to overtake the daylight. Captain Rojas did not appear. The rest of the convoy set up camp a kilometer from the wreck, but the Buick could still draw attention to the area. They were now in rebel territory, and the local townspeople and farmers would surely give away their positions to the enemy. The people in this region hated Batista and had already provided much aid and encouragement to Fidel and the rebels. As night quickly approached, the detail of four men that remained at the wreck with Rigo, all a part of his unit, set up a hasty defensive position.

Private Manuel Martinez was only seventeen. Like most teenagers in the Cuban Army, he was more scared than committed to the cause. He was the clown of the group, often compared to a giraffe because of his 6-foot 4-inch height, long neck, and awkward swagger.

Private Enrique Cortez was very proud and well-educated. He was pleased to announce that his great grandfather's lineage could be traced all the way back to Spain and a general in the Spanish army. This didn't sit well with most of the men, who viewed Spain as a cruel oppressor that attempted to kill the culture and traditions of their people. Stories were still shared on the island of Spanish General Valeriano Weyler, also known as The Butcher by the Cuban people and American reporters when they explained how he placed over 300,000 Cuban citizens in concentration camps after being named Governor of Cuba by Spain. Thousands of Cubans died in those camps, many of them of starvation and disease, and the rest at the hands of Weyler's men. Anyone accused of being a rebel against Spain's colonization suffered the same consequences.

Private First Class Vicente Fernandez's family leased a farm outside of Havana and sold sugarcane to the United Fruit Company. They had farmed the land for many generations. Vicente could trace his roots back to the slave trade with Africa. He was extremely dark and joked around with the other soldiers that his breeding had been on purpose and intended to create the finest fighter in the army.

Sergeant Third Class Pablo Flores was by far the most intelligent and professional soldier in the company. He was twenty-four years old and wanted to be the next Cuban weightlifting champion. At 230 pounds he could lift twice his weight and was literally strong as an ox. Loyal as he was strong, he had been in the Cuban army before the revolution and took satisfaction in defending the island.

Rigo was starting to regain his composure. He walked over to the creek to rinse off his hands and uniform. It would be more difficult to wash away the mental and emotional stains of the day. The flowing waters of the creek carried most of the blood and vomit away. He quietly sat on a large rock at the edge of the water, staring out at the Sierra Maestra Mountains in the distance. How could such majestic beauty and spiritual peace harbor the evilness of man? It was in these very places men gathered to plot deeds of hatred, greed, and murder. Often they cloaked their lust for power and wealth in the name of freedom and righteousness, as if this somehow could lessen the loss of life or human suffering inflicted on the common man. How many people had been annihilated and family members erased from photo albums in the quest for material possessions?

Rigo cleared his head and walked back to the men, now engaged in a discussion. The soldiers had been waiting to be picked up for several hours now.

Private Cortez got to his feet. "Lieutenant, why aren't they here to pick us up yet? El Capitan said he would come directly after they refueled. That was hours ago. What if something happened to them? I'm beginning to think the worst."

Private Fernandez smirked. "Don't go crazy, hombre, the capitan is more than pissed at the lieutenant for jumping down the cliff. He's making him wait to grind his balls a bit. I'm just glad to be here with the lieutenant. El Capitan will surely not leave his medic behind. I'm not so sure he'd return for the rest of us."

"What the hell do you mean? We're all good soldiers. Rojas will come back for all of us."

"Okay, Enrique, don't get your panties sweaty. The captain won't abandon us. But we need to make sure we survive the night. Hopefully

Fidel doesn't like American cars and finds out this used one has become recently available."

Sergeant Flores stood up. "Alright, ladies, enough talk. We're all on a long shit-list. Who gives a damn where the Captain is, what he thinks, or whether he remembers us or not? We have a job to do, to stay alive."

Rigo joined them. Flores turned to face him. "Isn't that right, Lieutenant?"

"Sergeant, you're almost always right when it comes to the men. Vamonos. We need to set up a perimeter. If the sun rises and we don't rise with it, it'll be because we weren't prepared. Sergeant, we need five foxholes in a horseshoe formation. Orient them to the south facing the creek. The car is a point of reference. I will dig my own foxhole in the middle and you and the men place two on each of my sides. Place the claymore mines in position just beyond the small bushes to the left and this side of the creek. Move, Sergeant, we have very little daylight left."

Cortez muttered, "I pray we aren't digging our graves."

Sergeant Flores issued commands, and the men moved quickly and got busy. Chatter was at a minimum. The only noise came from the entrenching tools that scraped the earth. The scraping, falling dirt, and the occasional sigh created a slightly off-key chorus as the men labored for the sole purpose of preserving their lives.

They didn't dig deep foxholes in the rocky earth, as that would have taken too many hours. The hasty defensive positions left the men partially exposed, but it was better than sitting on the road with limited visibility or moving at night in hostile territory.

Vicente moved seventy-five yards in front of the foxholes. He took a M18A1 claymore mine out of the green bandolier, opened the two metal scissor-leg stands, and put the mine in its predetermined place. About the size of a brick but only about an inch and a half thick, the convex green plastic case held a hundred steel balls that would explode over a 100 meters at a 60° arc. One mine could kill or wound an entire platoon of men. He was careful to look for the reminder imprinted on the front of the device, "FRONT TOWARD ENEMY." He spaced the mines some thirty yards from each other and created a 180-degree defensive fighting perimeter. Next he ran a wire connecting the devices and low crawled back to his foxhole, carefully running the wire like an umbilical cord to a newborn's navel. He cut the end of the wire and inserted it into the firing mechanism. The "clacker" resembled a two-inch stapler and was named for the noise it made when triggered.

As the night settled, the temperature dropped to sixty degrees. They had rolled down the sleeves of their olive drab fatigues, which was little comfort as the wind swept through the creek bed and valley. Sergeant Flores scheduled them to take sleep breaks but they were unable to do so because of their fear and the reality of vulnerability to the enemy. It was now after midnight and five hours of darkness had passed. They listened for sounds but only heard the wind howling through the creek bed. The mind and body can play tricks on a soldier facing potential dangers. On several occasions it looked like there was something moving along the creek. Manuel was the first to speak.

"Vicente. I see something. Look, just on the other side of the creek, northeast about two hundred yards. Something's moving out there."

"What, Manuel? I see nothing but a scared little boy."

"I may be scared, but I see something out there, I can feel it too."

Vicente looked out beyond the creek. "I see something too. Could be animals, maybe dogs, but don't make any noise. Keep your eyes on that area. I'll tell the others."

Vicente crawled over to Rigo's position. "Teniente, we see something moving across the creek. It isn't the trees, something's there."

Rigo scanned the area. "Where?"

Vicente pointed towards the area, but nothing was clearly visible. Rigo could tell something was out there but not discern if it was human or animal. "Don't assume they're rebels. The last thing we want to do is harm villagers or livestock. Continue to watch but do not fire until I give a command, understand? That's an order."

Vicente returned to his position.

Rigo low crawled to Flores's foxhole directly next to his own. "Look to the right, there appears to be some activity. We mustn't panic. Keep the men alert. Tell Cortez the same. He's not to fire unless I give the command. Is that clear?"

"Si, mi jefe."

Rigo returned to his hole and began to feel the seriousness of this situation. His first priority must be to remain calm and lead the men regardless of his own fear and uncertainty. He felt a sense of responsibility for putting the men in this potentially life-threatening situation. The same type of guilt he felt when Tony died in a hail of bullets in a casino parking lot. He learned through experience he wouldn't be any help to the men looking backwards on his life and decisions during critical moments. The curse of being a hardheaded Cuban wasn't lost on him. "Dios mio, please give me the strength to make good decisions tonight and forgive me for my ignorance and failures as a leader. Help us survive this situation, and I will promise to listen to your whispers as I pray you hear mine now." He could hear Cortez and Flores talking under their breath across the foxholes.

"Cortez! Listen, shithead, you fire without an order and I'll put a bullet in your stupid ass. Do not fire your weapon until ordered."

"I'm not dying tonight without fighting. This isn't my fight. I shouldn't be here in this shit."

"Keep it together, man. We're not in danger right now. If they're rebels, you'll only draw them to our positions. We lie low and hope they don't see us. Keep your damn voice down, whispers only."

"I see them, they're crossing the creek, I see them. I can take them. Let me kill those fuckers. You're all putas, I'll fight for my life."

Flores low crawled into the man's hole. Cortez had his gun aimed toward the creek and was moving his finger towards the trigger. Flores stood behind him and quickly wrapped an arm around his throat. He didn't release his grip until he felt the other man's body slide out of consciousness. He put Flores's weapon on safety, felt for his pulse, and pushed the unconscious solder to the side and assumed his position in the hole.

Rigo crawled over to where the men were lying motionless. "Que paso? There's too much noise here."

"He lost it, sir. He was going to fire, I had no choice but to calm him. I was just going to punch him, but then I thought he might fire or make noise, so I just choked the breath out of him. He'll wake up in a minute."

"When he wakes up, if he's still crazy with fear, sit on him, gag him, knock him out, but just keep him quiet."

Rigo crawled to Vicente's hole. "What do you see?"

"Three people moving behind the bushes. I can't tell if they're villagers looking at the wreck or rebel soldiers."

"We'll wait until we're sure. They haven't fired, and I can't believe they didn't hear Cortez. They could have heard him whining all the way to Havana. We'll know soon enough if they're Castro's men or farmers. Do not detonate the Claymores or fire until we're sure."

"Sir, there are now more than eight, maybe ten by the car and then the three in the bushes. I can get them. They're on the edge of the mine kill zones. Give me the order and I'll take them out." Vicente clearly did not like the uncertainty of the situation. They watched the shadows move. Some drifted away from the car and walked down the road.

"Do you see them, sir? If we don't fire, they'll be past the middle mine and kill zone sweet spot. Let me fire the mines, sir. It may be too late if we wait. We need to fire."

"Hold on, Vicente. Would a rebel patrol walk down the middle of a road?"

Three of the shadows moved into the bushes and they heard whistling. Were they taunting them? The men raised their M1s and clicked them off safety. Vicente released the safety on the clacker leading to the tethered mines and braced for the clack sound that would precede the violent explosion of steel and flesh. The cold night was now filled with sweat, fear, and silence. No one moved. They hardly dared to breathe.

And then, as if on a silent signal, the shadows began to move away from the road, and they could hear the splashing of feet in the creek. There was no immediate movement of Rigo's little fighting force. It seemed they had become one with their weapons, one with the night, with the sounds of the shadows moving steadily distant. Finally, as if a cold wind had swept ashore from the sea, the night regained its silence, and hope returned that they would live to see the morning.

However, Rigo did not relax. He low crawled past the foxholes, crept along the road, and listened to hear if the shadows weren't really retreating but only slithering further down the road to flank them. The silence remained.

They didn't sleep that night, except for Cortez. Thankfully, the sun began to rise over the mountains. Rigo knew they could not waste time getting out of the valley. "Vicente, remove the Claymores and prepare to move out of this position."

"Very well, sir. What will we do?"

"How is Cortez doing?" Rigo asked. "Did you kill him, or do we need to bring him back to camp?"

Flores grinned. "He's fine, sir. I let him sleep. We had a nice chat about the meaning of life. Especially duty, following orders, and teamwork, so you don't need to concern yourself with him. He'll do better next time. However, unless it rained last night, I think he pissed his pants."

Rigo slung the M1 over his shoulder. "I'd say every real soldier pisses his pants one time or another."

Vicente placed his arm through the shoulder strap of his M1 and let it dangle on his back as he crawled over to the first of the mines. "Holy shit! Sir, get over here, you have to see this."

Rigo crawled over to Vicente and read the writing on the mine. "FRONT TOWARD ENEMY." Except now, it was facing towards them. Flores crawled over to the second mine, and the third. All of them had been turned to face towards them.

Rigo shook his head. "Men, we owe our lives to our confusing enemy. They knew we were here. If they'd fired on us, we would have blown the mines and sliced ourselves to pieces. We were a second away from making our debut in hell."

"Why would they do that, sir?"

Rigo only stared out towards the mountains.

"Maybe they saw Rigo trying to save the farmer," Flores said. "Maybe they had no taste for blood last night."

Rigo started winding up the cords that connected the mines. "Maybe because we're all Cubans at heart when it comes down to it. Well, men, we know this village and this road belong to Castro. If we stay here talking like old women we may yet meet our maker today. Gather your gear and let's get the hell out of here. We need to be on the road above the cliff in ten."

They learned much about themselves and their enemy that night. Certainly the rebels were still their enemy in war and politics. They were, however, united for at least one moment of potential mercy. Those rebel soldiers showed honor, and faith in a Cuban future. Possibly, just possibly, they were much like Rigo and his men but just saw some things differently.

CHAPTER SEVEN

Stop the Bleeding

The five men scurried to the small path leading to the road. Slowly they wound their way up out of the valley and onto the road. Manuel was in front with Rigo and Cortez, while Flores and Vicente held the rear. After the nighttime encounter, Rigo ordered them to maintain proper distance, keep their weapons locked and loaded, and be on the lookout for anything out of the ordinary. Sergeant Flores relayed the Lieutenant's orders. "We're headed in the same direction as the men we saw last night. I want to get to camp in one piece. I'm looking forward to a conversation with our capitan. So be alert, cut the chatter, focus."

If they traveled on foot all the way to the camp, there was a strong possibility they'd encounter rebels. With Vicente at the rear keeping watch behind them while Cortez did the same in front, they all took positions on the side of the road. After an hour had passed, Cortez said, "Car." They soon heard the sound of an engine and saw dust rising on the road ahead. Rigo signaled to Flores with his arm extended and hand in a slicing up and down motion and pointed to the middle of the road. Flores stood up, moved to the middle of the road, and pointed his rifle directly at the oncoming vehicle. The Chevrolet's driver quickly stopped, creating a cloud of dust and debris all around the car. Flores approached the driver.

"In the name of the Cuban government, I ask that you step out of this vehicle and surrender it to Company C of the Eighteenth Battalion. Now! Move!"

"Que pasa, muchacho? I'm a Cuban citizen. You can't take my car." The villager reluctantly stepped out of the car.

"I just did. Now move out of my way. Contact your precinct to get your car back." Flores gently pushed the man to one side and away from the driver's door. He signaled to the rest of the men. They emerged from the side of the road and jumped into the car, each keeping watch on the road until it was his turn to get in. Rigo was the last to get in and sat in the front passenger seat.

Manuel took the wheel. "Is this the best you could do? A Chevy sedan? Next time let's wait for a Buick."

Cortez laughed. "Sergeant Flores, where did you get that line, 'in the name of the Cuban government?' I felt the presence of Presidente Batista himself as you spoke."

"Enough chatter," Flores said. "Keep your eyes on the road front, back, and sides."

The Chevrolet's V8 roared and Manuel drove as fast as possible on the winding road. The hairpin turns required slowing down to a virtual crawl in order to avoid falling off a cliff like the unfortunate young farmer the day before.

Rigo broke the silence. "Manuel, be sure to speed up as soon as we make these crazy turns. We don't want to be moving slow in this area. Keep your eyes alert, men. Take the triggers off safety and make sure the rifles are pointed out the window."

"We look like Cuban gangsters with our big Chevrolet and weapons sticking out every window," Manuel said. "Like the Al Capones of Havana."

Flores kept his rifle pointed out of the backseat side window. He didn't take his eyes off the road as he spoke "Just drive, hombre."

When they approached the area where the rebels had been headed the prior evening, no one said a word for over ten minutes. Rigo lifted himself slightly off the seat and locked his eyes onto something ahead. "Look to the right, men. Three o'clock, three o'clock! Men moving at the tree line. Manuel, step on it. Go, go, go!"

Bullets ricocheted off the side of the car. Rigo and Cortez opened fire into the woods on the right. Manuel gripped the steering wheel and floored the gas. Several men in olive drab fatigues and caps ran for cover, bullets blazed past the vehicle, some clanked into the side and rear of the car, rubber and dust spun from the tires. The rebels kept firing at the fleeing vehicle. Rigo could see the muzzle flashes in the rearview mirror through the hole where the rear window use to be.

Manuel squeezed the steering wheel even more tightly and let out a controlled scream. "Hijo de puta, I'm hit!"

Rigo flicked his weapon on safety and grabbed the steering wheel with his left hand. Manuel slumped back in the seat, bleeding profusely from the right side of his chest. He let go of the steering wheel, the car slowed, the fire from the rebels increased with new vigor.

Rigo pushed his foot down on top of Manuel's. The car swerved down the road and picked up speed. Flores had not stopped laying down cover fire to the rear. Manuel's blood, the careening vehicle, and the necessity of creating space between them and the ambush filled Rigo's mind. Tending Miguel's injury would have to wait until they were safely out of range.

Did the rebels have vehicles in the woods or up ahead? Were they being herded into a kill zone worse than the one they were trying to escape?

They drove on for a few miles until they had a direct line of sight in both directions and could see behind them over a mile. They looked back to see if the rebels were following and then ahead, but only a tractor and two farmers appeared in the distance. Rigo said, "Do you need ammo? Give Flores all of Manuel's and whatever clips you all have left. Flores, redistribute all of the ammunition." Rigo drove the car as fast as he could for another couple of minutes until they had passed the farmers on the tractor and then applied the brakes, steering the car towards a small shoulder area on the right side of the road.

Barely to a complete stop, Rigo grabbed the gearshift lever and slammed the car into park. He jumped out of the passenger side, sped over to the driver's door, and opened the door. The boy soldier slumped backwards on the seat. "Manuel, can you hear me?" He lifted him by the collar of his fatigue blouse and dragged him slowly around the front of the car to a spot on the ground away from the road. He quickly tore open Manuel's shirt. The other men, without being ordered, set up defensive positions along the roadside.

Blood from the wound in Manuel's chest seeped between Rigo's fingers. He lifted his bloody right hand and signaled Fernandez to come over. "Put some pressure on this wound so I can get a dressing ready." Thankfully, through all this Manuel remained unconscious. Fernandez knelt over the prone body. "Put your hands here," Rigo said, "and press down, hard, to stop the flow of blood." Fernandez pressed down.

"Let's go, man," Rigo said to Manuel. "You got too much to live for. Breathe, man breathe!" His voice trembled but he remained in control. "Manuel, fight. We need you, man. Damn it, you're too young, too young." The blood continued to leak through his fingers and down his arm, refusing to stop oozing.

Fernandez continued to apply pressure. "Lieutenant, I don't know what to do, I can't stop the bleeding. Don't die hombre, don't die!"

"You're doing fine, just fine, Fernandez. I've almost got this together, hold him upright." He replaced his hand over the wound as Fernandez removed his own blood-soaked hand. Rigo felt around Manuel's back then pulled his KA-BAR combat knife from his belt and set it on Manuel's stomach. "There is no exit wound, this should work. Hold him still. I need you to kneel behind him and wrap your arms around his torso. Be sure to hold his wrist tightly. He'll certainly move as I do this."

Rigo pulled out his lighter and let the flame flicker against the knife blade. He stared at the hole in Manuel's chest and tried to wipe up some of the excess blood around it so he could see what he was doing. Once the blade was searing hot, he held it parallel to the wound and slowly began to run the tip around the perimeter of the hole in Manuel's chest. Manuel jerked up several times in agony. Rigo had to reheat the blade and return to the wound, pressing the knife onto another side of it. Manuel clenched and contorted for several seconds then went limp. The bleeding began to slow.

Rigo placed a gauze patch over the bullet hole with the seared edges and soaked up more of the blood from the area. Fernandez took a bottle of alcohol from the first aid bag and, as instructed by Rigo, poured it on the lieutenant's left hand. Rigo shook the excess liquid from his hand and placed two fingers in the open wound pushing his fingers deeper, reaching for the bullet that had pierced Manuel's subclavian artery. After several minutes of feeling around the loose tissue and veins of the 17-year-old, a bloody bullet popped out and landed on the road, still steaming from the heat created as the projectile entered Manuel's chest and rested in his organs.

Rigo now had to treat the open wound. The bleeding had intensified. He again plunged his fingers into the hole. Manuel convulsed repeatedly, a sign that his body was reacting to the pain and loss of blood. Rigo knew he had only a short time before the artery would pump out so much blood that it would take the life of the young soldier. Even if he could stop the bleeding, he had to get Manuel to the field clinic where they would begin to replace some of the fluid. He searched for what seemed like an eternity, going deeper in the chest, reaching and contorting his hands in search of the pulsating vein. After several minutes he said, "Quick, get a clasp out of the bag." Fernandez took out what appeared to be a pair of scissors and handed the artery forceps to Rigo. With one hand Rigo buried the tip of the instrument into the open wound and what looked like a blood-soaked piece of yarn. He could see the pulsing artery still spurting and a chunk missing from the damage inflicted by the bullet. "Not today, Manuel, not today. You will not die today."

He felt at that moment he was responsible for Manual's soul and owned the burden of keeping him alive. If he couldn't save this man's life, he would have to live with the decision he made that led to this for the rest of his existence on earth. His decision to leap off a cliff against orders had placed all of these men in jeopardy and the weight of that moment had a surreal effect on him. He felt a power from someplace deep inside. Not of his own strength, but that of a guiding presence leading him forward. Thoughts of Tony and how he felt weak and powerless as his cousin died in front of him only increased his focus as if there was another hand controlling his own.

Rigo squeezed the handle of the medical instrument and as he did, it made a distinctive snap. The blood stopped spurting. Rigo poured the alcohol remaining in the bottle over the wound. He then cleaned it with medical bandages, covered it with a field dressing, and wrapped it tightly with gauze holding the handle of the forceps steady and securely in place on his chest. There was no need to check the pulse. Rigo could feel Manuel's heart beating as he held the vein in his hand. He was still alive but had lost a lot of blood.

"Let's go, men, let's go! Be careful not to touch the bandages. Flores, you drive. Avoid fast turns or holes in the road. Vicente, you get in the back with Manuel. Place his head in your lap. Watch the wound. Keep him from moving if he wakes up. Cortez, you sit in the rear and cover our asses, keep your eyes on the tree line too. If you see anything, don't hesitate to light it up." In unison the men responded. "Si, teniente."

The men didn't speak while they carried out Rigo's orders. As they headed towards the camp in San Luis, Rigo noticed the low-fuel light turn on.

CHAPTER EIGHT

Campo Militar San Luis

Rigo checked the distances on the map and estimated the speed that would bring them safely to the camp. "Vicente, keep it at thirty. Manuel is stable, the blood stopped seeping into the bandages. We'll be good at that speed. Unless the rebels have faster vehicles."

As the men approached the first checkpoint on the outskirts of the base, two guards walked in front of the barricades and stopped them. One went to the passenger side and one to the driver's side. The soldiers recognized the rank on Rigo's uniform and saluted. They noticed the soldier lying in the back seat covered in blood with a pair of scissors clamped to his chest.

"Que paso, mi teniente?"

Rigo briefly explained then added, "Radio the doctor we're on the way with an injured soldier. And we 're going to need one of your gas cans in case we run out on the road."

"Lift the gate. Yes sir, we'll take care of that right now."

As the men drove through the barricade they heard the squawk on the radio. At the other end of the barricade, one of the guards loaded two jerrycans of gas into the trailing jeep that now escorted the band of soldiers from Company C.

The remaining 11 miles to the camp in San Luis, at 45 miles an hour, seemed like an eternity. Manuel's blood pressure remained low. Vicente kept talking to Manuel in the back seat, but Manuel remained unresponsive. He appeared to be in a coma-like state, and his skin was ashen. Occasionally Rigo would glance into the backseat and be overcome with sadness.

The guard's radio message described the situation and type of vehicle that would be approaching and alerted the next two checkpoints to simply wave the vehicles through.

"Sir, the last checkpoint's coming up, and we should be about a mile from the infirmary," Vincente said.

"Good, we have a chance to keep him alive. Flores, how's he doing?"

"Barely breathing and making noises like a Moka coffee pot before it boils, like a gurgle."

"The blood's making its way into his lungs. Pulmonary edema can kill him. We don't have much time. The doctor will need to open his chest to drain the blood. Sit him upright and make sure his airway is clear so he doesn't choke on his own blood." Flores grabbed Manuel's shirt and hoisted his body up against him. It reminded Rigo of how he held onto another person, bleeding, dying for no good reason, in a Havana hotel parking lot. Death was now a part of his daily imagery, occupying more time than he cared for, and slowly corrupting his belief in God, humanity, and hope for his country.

Rigo stared out the window. The captain was wrong to leave them, but he himself was wrong when he put everyone at risk by leaping down the cliff. Maybe he shouldn't be an officer who leads men and risks their lives. He wanted to be a medic and help people, not hurt people in the process. Now he ended up being the one who caused pain to others. Was he so messed up he could think only of the moment? He should have made better decisions. Always trying to prove himself. Who did he need to prove himself to? God? His father? That dick wasn't even man enough to stay around. His madre, America? He didn't think he could ever do enough to make her happy. She only saw his mistakes, and there'd been plenty, enough for her to lose trust in him. Juanita was his saving grace, and his only good decision was holding onto and loving her.

Dios mio, he must stop hurting people! Juanita doesn't deserve to live in a world with a broken man fighting a revolution no one can win. Maybe he should have pushed her away like the others that got too close. But it was impossible with Juanita. He saw her and knew that there was something different in her eyes and her soul. He wanted to have her. She had his heart immediately. She became the better part of them when together and always on his mind when apart. He desperately wanted to be a part of her life story. It should be a beautiful one about raising and chasing their children on the farm and not what they have experienced in this useless revolution.

If he lost Manuel on this road, he'd never be able to forgive himself. He would become one of those men conquered by his own past. He would eventually lose Juanita to that man. The one who couldn't bear the ugly scar of failure and instead had embraced self-loathing. He wouldn't be able to look at her without hiding something she should never know. This would be his pain and his alone. But he wanted to see that look in her eyes once more that said her trust was complete and he was still her hero.

He remembered the mornings and sunsets that belonged to them. Days they existed only for themselves. Long embraces and spontaneous kisses. These moments were the strength that allowed him to push through temporary physical and emotional pain. He thought of Francisco and Carlos, their beautiful boys. Rigo had had no father to teach him, no map to show him how to be what he had so deeply wanted as a child. But he had done the best he could. He was driven to become everything his own father had not been.

Yet he had become what he did not want to be, a distant father, not around while his sons grew up. Had it been worth it, fighting against a revolution for a government that did not listen to the voices of the very people it existed for? Maybe he was no better than his father—

Bullets hit the ground in front of the car. The guards at the camp gate had opened fire on them!

Flores slammed on the brakes. "What the hell!"

Vicente grabbed hold of Manuel and yanked him behind the front seat, draping his body over Manuel's, creating a human barrier between the injured soldier and oncoming bullets.

"Shit, we've driven into a trap, the rebels have taken the camp. They're rebels… they must be rebels…" Flores raised his hands. "Hold your fire! Don't kill us!"

Rigo yelled, "Don't shoot! I'm Lieutenant Gonzales of Company C Eighteenth Battalion!"

"Please, in the name God, don't shoot," Flores said. "We have an injured soldier and must get him to the doctor or he'll die."

The two guards appeared no older than Manuel, visibly shaking and unsure of themselves as they cautiously approached the car with their rifles aimed. Teenage boys, not one single hair on their faces was visible. They looked inside the jeep and recognized Rigo's lieutenant bar and officer rank.

"Oh my God, Lieutenant, we almost killed you! We got a garbled transmission from the front guard checkpoint. It was incomplete and inaudible. We only heard bits like, 'Be alert for a car with armed men coming your way.' Forgive us, sir, please!"

"Enough shit!" screamed Flores. "Get out of our way or you'll be joining us in the infirmary. Move, now!"

"Yes, sergeant," said the younger guard.

Rigo glanced into the back seat. Manuel had opened his eyes! "Muchacho! Can you hear me? Manuel can you hear me? Stay with us, muchacho."

Manuel remained silent but awake and winced in pain. It might have been better if he'd stayed unconscious. When he tried to move, Vicente held him tight. "Don't move, hombre. You don't want to loosen what the lieutenant has done. Stay calm. We're getting you help." Manuel groaned and closed his eyes.

Flores clutched a hand to his own heart. "Is he dead?"

Vicente patted Manuel on the head. "Just resting. Fighting for his life."

The men now pulled into Camp San Luis, a temporary camp consisting mostly of tents and military vehicles. The vehicles on the road had their lights illuminating the Cuban night that had begun to overtake the day. Some of the soldiers of Company C were preparing to run patrols. There were few soldiers visible except those cleaning weapons or on guard duty around the perimeter. Rigo pointed Flores to the tent with the Cuban Flag and first aid cross. The car came to a complete stop a few feet in front of the tent. A nurse outside of the tent immediately pointed in the direction of the field operating room. The men in the car quickly and gently removed Manuel, put him on a stretcher, and whisked him inside the tent. Rigo and the men walked in with them and passed two other injured soldiers who had already been bandaged.

The men laid the stretcher on an open table beneath bright lights that illuminated the seriousness of the wound. Another nurse appeared and began undressing Manuel. The nurses were dressed more like nuns and looked as if all their beauty had been sucked out of them by their current circumstances. Only in their late twenties or early thirties, their weathered faces reflected pain, not physical but emotional, brought on by absorbing the pains of others. Even so, the men looked at them with desire. After many days or months in the jungle, the smell and touch of a woman was intoxicating. For Rigo it was simply a reminder of Juanita.

The doctor, a major in the Cuban Army, pulled Rigo aside. "What happened?"

Rigo explained the wound, his actions to treat it, and Manuel's subsequent condition.

The doctor nodded. "We'll get to work on him now, I'll let you know as soon as we find out if there's other damage and if he's going to make it."

"I'll send the men out," Rigo said, "but I'm staying with him until he's well enough to tell me to leave."

"Listen to me, Lieutenant. I'm telling, not asking. You've done a lot to help. It's now in God's hands and hopefully he leads us in his work. You're visibly tired and shaken. You won't be any help to your friend now. Trust me in this matter. Go. Go and rest."

Rigo turned his gaze to the ground before looking at the doctor again. He reflected on his recent rash actions and quick decisions, especially how they had impacted others. He captured his anger-filled words before they escaped. "As you say, sir." The men exited the makeshift operating room.

As Rigo turned and walked away, a tear developed and started to accumulate. He wished it might be rain. He couldn't explain, even to himself, how he felt at this moment. His thoughts returned to the reality of their mission and he wiped a blood-caked sleeve across his face.

The men waited for him just outside the tent's common area. He spotted a sergeant. "Sergeant, do you know where I can find Capitan Rojas? We have some military business to discuss."

CHAPTER NINE

The Rebels Yell

"Liberty is the right of every man to be honest about who he is and what his dreams are, to think and to speak beyond hypocrisy."

-Jose Marti

The sergeant faltered briefly before responding. "He's in the village, interrogating the local farmworkers. He'll be back by nightfall."

"Thank you, Sergeant." The other three soldiers no doubt hoped Rigo remembered he was a lieutenant and the commander a captain. There was no telling which one of them would explode first.

Rigo walked back to the officers' tent reflecting on the last 48 hours and reminding himself not to lose his temper. That might be exactly what the captain wanted. What reasonable explanation was there for leaving five men with no support overnight in hostile territory? His hatred for Rigo must run deeper than he imagined.

Rigo headed to the latrine and shower area. He thought about simply walking into the shower fully clothed and washing away all the dirt and filth of the last 48 hours, but he paused in front of the mirror for several seconds and noticed how much he had aged. He was too young a man to start seeing clumps of gray hair. He looked down at his hands, still blotched and tinted with Manuel's dark red blood. He began to clean and scrub his hands as well as his shirtsleeves. He scrubbed so hard his nails punctured his own flesh. He had attempted to erase and clean away the stains and memories but instead only inflicted more wounds.

The double-sized tent made of green seasoned canvas reeked of cigars and sunbaked perspiration. It was large enough for twelve men but served as lodging for only four officers. This was one of the small benefits of being a leader in the Cuban military. A guard stood posted at the opening of the tent and greeted everyone who entered with a salute. Rigo returned the salute and proceeded through the small opening. He found two older men huddled around a map. One of the men was First Sergeant Tomas Lucha of Company C, a career soldier who had spent over 30 years in the Cuban Army. Lucha had seen 14 presidents come into power in Cuba beginning with Gerardo Machado in 1928. He spoke his mind and was hardened by life and his chosen career. The other man was the executive officer, First Lieutenant Sardina, who was reserved and slow to speak but a good soldier and military thinker.

"Buenos dias, caballeros," Rigo said.

"Thank God, man, you're here." Sardina patted Rigo on the back. "We thought you were dead or captured. What happened?"

Rigo told them the story and looked at the first sergeant. "Why didn't the captain come to pick us up last night? We should all be dead by now."

First Sergeant Lucha responded before the last word left Rigo's mouth. "Sir, the capitan did not leave you to your fate. He sent a team out last night with two jeeps to find you and the men and bring you in safely. Unfortunately, they never made it to you. We lost contact with them as darkness fell. Sir, permission to speak freely?"

"Please do."

"He sent men out against my recommendation. He's now in the village trying to gather intelligence on the rebels' whereabouts and our missing soldiers. I told him he should have left you at the bottom of the cliff. You put a lot of men and this operation at risk by your macho bullshit. You're a medic, not a fucking hero. That's what's on my mind, sir."

Lt. Sardina swallowed hard but did not take his gaze off the first sergeant while awaiting Rigo's response. He was probably glad Rigo hadn't already lunged at the sergeant. He'd once seen Rigo beat a man for simply bumping into him after a night of drinking in Havana. Rigo had an explosive temperament and a reputation for not taking kindly to criticism. It was a very long ten seconds.

Rigo looked hard at the sergeant. "You're right. I put men at risk and went against the judgment of our leader. I offer no defense for my actions and will fully accept my consequences. I simply saw someone who needed help. My biggest regret is that others suffered far more than I did for my actions. But let's be clear on something. We can talk like men in here as equals, but I don't want to hear you speaking of my actions in front of the men or calling my leadership into question. Am I clear?"

The sergeant bowed his head. "Crystal clear, sir. Conversation over."

"I'm going to check on Manuel," Rigo said, "and then I'll be in the command tent. I'll wait for the captain there. We may not have heard the end of the rebels today. They appear to be concentrating in this area. They don't respect our strength anymore and may soon probe the camp for weaknesses. Every soldier must be prepared to defend this post. First

Sergeant, check the perimeter and ensure we're not caught with our pants down."

"Si, Lieutenant." He saluted and left the tent.

Rigo turned to Sardina as he stared at the floor watching a military formation of ants carry a large crumb of bread. "What are you thinking, my friend?"

"Soldiers in battle often carry the burden of war for the sake of gaining something. Even in victory it's often for the benefit of others. Like with these ants. The queen and princess ants are the ones who benefit from the hard labor of these soldiers and workers. Have we advanced less than these creatures? We still use soldiers to kill others and carry away the fallen crumbs left by those who had the misfortune of bad aim. It's sad. Sad and tragically funny."

Rigo walked out of the tent trying desperately to clear his head and find the words to explain his actions to the captain. He shouldn't have assumed the worst about him. Rojas sent soldiers out to find them, risking men and the mission. Once again he had rushed to judgment without sufficient consideration. He must now turn his hateful thoughts into those of appreciation and personal responsibility. Regardless of what happened to him, he must own his actions and make things right.

As he walked toward the medical tent, the capitan's jeep rolled through the security gate. Rigo changed his direction away from the medical unit to the command tent. He didn't see the grenade hit the guard shack, he only felt the vibration as the explosion destroyed the shack and the two young guards manning their post.

The second grenade landed inside the jeep waiting to enter the camp, instantly killing two more soldiers. Captain Rojas was ejected out the back seat of his jeep and was airborne for what seemed like an eternity. The men from C Company, taken by surprise, started to empty their tents. Guerillas charged at them from the jungle. Bullets raged in every direction. Several bodies hit the dirt. Rigo, now prone on the ground, could see Capitan Rojas lying still next to the shattered jeep. He had no weapon and no way to defend himself. The hundred yards between the Jeep and where Rigo lay seemed like the entire length of the island of Cuba.

Ignoring the sound of pain around him, he jumped to his feet, zigzagged through the machinegun fire that filled the camp with the metallic smell of gunpowder and death, and ran.

He closed the gap to about thirty yards when he saw four men heading towards the captain from the jungle. He slipped behind a group of palm trees near where the guard shack once stood. A dead rebel lay with his Cristobal automatic rifle at his side. Rigo leapt towards the weapon then fell back into a prone position. He aimed at the men, held his breath, and slowly squeezed the trigger. The first round entered the lead soldier, who hit the ground. The next three rounds took the other men. Without a thought he leaped to his feet and sprinted towards the captain.

The first thing he noticed was the three-inch piece of metal protruding from the captain's back. The next thing he noticed were three rebels running towards them from the jungle. The captain's driver was in the mangled vehicle 20 feet from the captain, still alive after the blast. He reached for his rifle and took aim at the charging men. Two of the rebels fell as a bullet entered the eye socket of the first and the base of the neck of the second. This was the last thing the soldier did here on earth.

The third rebel was only a few steps away from Rigo and the captain when he fell forward like a baseball player sliding headfirst into second base. Sergeant Flores appeared out of nowhere kneeling directly in front of them, his rifle still pointed at the falling rebel.

Metal and smoke filled the air and the rattle of weapons vibrated and rang in Rigo's ears. All around him were screams and explosions. A bullet entered Flores's thigh. He lay ten feet away.

Rigo hefted the capitan by his armpits and dragged him toward Flores. A prone Cuban soldier yelled and pointed his rifle towards the opening in the jungle as more rebels moved in on them. Rigo pulled Rojas by his shirt collar towards the C Company soldiers now forming a defensive fighting position. He'd come back for Flores once he reached a secure location for Rojas. Rojas was unconscious and merely a passenger as the men moved together towards the inner part of the camp. The fighting was occurring on the perimeter of the compound while the Cuban soldiers took positions in a semicircle in front of the command tent.

Rigo dragged the captain to the medical tent parallel to the command tent. Across the dimly lit tent, mostly illuminated by the bullet holes that formed a pattern of sunlight, the doctor worked on a wounded soldier. Rigo carefully rested the captain on his stomach. "Here's El Capitan. Please don't let him die. Get the doctor over here quickly."

Rigo left the tent and headed towards Flores, but the big Cuban was no longer there. He saw a soldier on the ground 20 yards away and recognized Cortez's silhouette. He needed to get Cortez away from the perimeter's barrage of gunfire. As he approached, he noticed another young man leaning against a tree and holding his side and stomach. Rigo moved to the injured man and began to examine his injuries. At that instant the man suddenly pulled a pistol from his waistband and aimed it at Rigo. Another rebel appeared from behind the tree, pointed his weapon at Rigo and shouted, "Manos ariba, hijo de puta!"

Rigo raised his hands, not over his head, but at shoulder level with his palms facing the rebels. He only saw the butt of the rifle for a split second before it crashed into his temple.

CHAPTER TEN

The Bearer of News is Not My Friend

"Let the people who judged you see how I cherish you now, let those who condemn you see how close you are to me."

-Anonymous

The knock on her door brought hopeful anticipation. Maybe Rigo had returned, his mission with the army done, but then he wouldn't knock. Reality and fear greeted her at the front door in the form of Pedro Ponce, a sad looking man, the town's vice mayor and a longtime friend of the family. His bushy eyebrows hid his focus as his eyes stared down at the ground.

"Hola, America, I have some news of your son, Rigo. I'm afraid it isn't the good news you pray for, but you should know it anyway. I'm truly sorry and saddened. This letter comes from the rebel command. I was asked to read it so that I know you were offered a way to help him in case you choose to do nothing."

America swallowed hard and breathed deeply. Her heart raced with crippling fear and uncontrolled anticipation. She prepared herself, knowing Pedro's words would alter the direction of her life. She squeezed the side of her long blue faded dress and put her hands on her hips as she looked up at Pedro with a penetrating gaze. "Que es, hombre?"

"He's been captured and is unaccounted for by his company. Some of the men saw him dragged away by rebels, but they don't know what happened to him after that. He was on the southern side of the island, close to the Sierra Maestra."

America hung on every word, wanting to change the message yet repeating it to herself, trying to grasp what it really meant. "Dragged away? Was he, is he, alive?" She had more questions but could not find the words.

In the quiet, neither one of them made eye contact. Pedro handed her a letter.

Señora America Gonzalez,

We have your son, Rigo. He is a member of the Batista Army that is responsible for looting and enslaving the free people of Cuba. He deserves to die, but we will graciously spare his life for $10,000 American dollars. This is a small price to pay for a life and to help support the future for all Cuban people. You have two days before your son, a traitor to the cause of Cuban independence, will die.

America held the letter to her heart, still processing the last two words. She gathered her composure and shook the old man's withered hand even while her own trembled with fear. He tried to withdraw it after the customary farewell, but she held fast.

"Thank you for coming. Pedro, I know you're busy in these difficult times. But I need more details. It's not enough only to know he was alive. Did he survive being captured? Where he is now? We all know what'll happen if I send them the money. He'll be killed anyway. Pedro, you must find this information for me. You know the people in the village and they'll talk to you. I'll do anything to know if he's still alive and where he's being held."

"America, I know you're sick with what I've told you, but it's all I know. The people who know more all support Castro. They'll want money before they say anything. Once you give them the money, they may tell you, but it's not guaranteed to be true. Time is also a problem, none more so than for your son."

"I'll cut my hand off with a machete, shake the hand of Castro himself with my severed hand! He may one day rule Cuba, but not my family. Find out if Rigo is alive and unharmed. If God grant me that, I'll do the rest."

"What will you do with this information?" Pedro said. "Even if he's alive, he's a prisoner. God knows where they may have taken him."

She walked to the kitchen where she kept her valuables in a small safe buried below a floorboard underneath the old stove. The safe had a Cuban Flag imprinted on it, but it was not really a safe. It was the size of a shoebox made of metal with a small lock protecting its contents.

She took out half of all the cash it possessed, seven thousand pesos, and returned the safe to its hiding place. She moved briskly back to the living room where Pedro fidgeted nervously. "Take this. I have to trust you. You have the power to be good to my family."

"I'll do everything I can. I'll come back tomorrow evening."

"Thank you."

She felt a wave of emotions but waited until he stepped outside and she slowly closed the door before her eyes produced tears. She must endure these feelings to stay strong for her son. She fell to the floor holding her stomach, now tightening and convulsing. There was no holding back the tears, and she released a wailing scream. Her body belonged to the fear of losing love again.

The next evening at 8:00, America's heartbeats quickened when she saw a shadow in the moonlight approaching the farmhouse. The dirt road leading to her casa was narrow and still wet from the late afternoon rains. The figure was walking down the middle of the road at a brisk pace. America swung open the front door. As Pedro become visible in the light from the front room, America searched for an emotion on his face. She didn't see gladness in his eyes. "Que paso, Pedro?"

"I have some news from the rebel supporters in the village. The sister of Marco Silva, one of Castro's captains, was told of an attack on Campo Militar San Luis. It was difficult to have to pay this woman for this; she wanted everything, all the money you gave me, before she'd say anything. It's especially hard when you know the money will surely go to help the rebels and hurt our own soldiers—"

"Pedro, we can save this talk for later? Where's my son? Is he alive?"

"Rigo was captured during the attack on his camp. A few of the men recognized him from Pinal Del Rio. He was taken prisoner but is still alive."

America sat down on her sofa. A single tear fell. "He's alive." She took her first soothing breath in a long time. "Thank you, God! How can—"

"Wait, please, let me finish. He's being held in a camp somewhere in the Sierra Maestra. She wouldn't tell me where, but it can't be far from San Luis."

"This is at least some good news, Pedro. She didn't tell you anything else because she wants more money. I know these people." She stood up. "Let's go see her now. I have a bit more money and gold. If it's not enough, I can bring my sugarcane machete and cut it out of her."

Pedro flinched and took a step back. "There's more. I won't mince my words. The rebels have a three-day rule. If they can't get information from a prisoner or money or the release of one of their own, they execute the prisoner at the end of the third day."

America processed Pedro's statement. "So I have forty-eight hours left to find Rigo."

"America, I know you're a fighter, but what can you do here in Havana? The army is looking for the rebels but can't find them. The area he's in strongly supports Castro. You must pray they find him soon, but there's no way for you to do anything at this point."

The lines in America's aging face tightened. "Pedro, all I ask of you is to tell me where the greedy witch lives."

"I've already risked a lot getting you this information. I have my own family to think of."

"I understand. Thank you for what you've done so far. I won't ask more of you. Where can I find her?"

Pedro stared at her for a long moment, scribbled a name and address on the back of an envelope, then walked back into the night.

The idea of the government staying intact was improbable. The work she put into the farms and their financial security would soon vanish as the rebels grew in strength and numbers. While many still held onto the possibility of a Batista victory, others were greedily taking advantage of fast-swelling fear and buying up property for next to nothing. That's whom she must find.

By midafternoon the next day, America returned to the farm after meeting with both a buyer for the farms and the rebel informant, a soldier who was injured in combat and was in desperate need of money. Sixteen hours had passed since she'd met with Pedro. She had less than 32 hours to find her son and do whatever was required to gain Rigo's release.

She arranged a ride with Jose, a farmhand and part-time taxi driver. The eight-hour drive to Bayamo would give her time to think and pray.

CHAPTER ELEVEN

America's Resolve

A merica knew her life would never be the same after this evening. She held 10,000 pesos in her right hand from selling the farms. She traveled around the house extracting money from all her hiding places. She got down on her hands and knees and took out the large envelope wedged into the bedsprings. She even emptied the old cigar box that held the remnants of her memories, the last gambling money from her late husband. Her hands were shaking not from fear but from determination.

She left enough to pay the week's wages to her workers and stuffed the rest in the front pocket of her white button-down sweater. She finally went to her little safe under the floorboard and took the remaining 7000 pesos. In total she had 25,000 pesos. America retrieved a pouch from her dresser and placed it on the left side of her hip, inside her underwear, in case she needed more money to bribe yet another rebel bastard. Twenty-five thousand pesos and five gold coins she had buried in the back yard. This was all of it. She had nothing else left.

"This is for you, you bastards in bed with Castro." She looked out the window at the dusty town. "And this is for you." She flashed a gesture of contempt at the vacant street. "I grew up with all of you and now you turn your back on me." In truth and deep inside she didn't blame them. They had no faith in Batista nor the Americans. Then she shouted out the window, "When this is all over you'll live a pathetic existence and feel ashamed for abandoning our government and leaders to support an armed tyrant! When all your freedoms are gone, and they take away your radios because they claim American baseball is propaganda, don't complain!"

Since she would be gone when Juanita returned from the city, she got out a pencil and a piece of paper and wrote her a letter.

Mi Nina, I doubt you have had any success trying to convince the government to do anything about Rigo. They are trying to save their own sorry asses and get as much money out of the country as they can before the jungle rats parade them down the Calle Principal. Tomorrow, just stay in my house here with the children. There is enough food here for you and the boys. The time for asking questions is over! Our government is running around like a chicken with its head cut off! They see us women as only a burden to be brushed away and dismissed. They do not know the tears of a mother or wife. I go now on this night with hope and fear.

I know where they have him, mi hija. Time is not our friend and I must hurry if there is any chance of saving his life. You must stay here with Francisco and Carlos. I do not know when and if I will return to see you. Please tell my little busy bees that I do love them dearly and hope to see them soon. Do not lose hope! I am prepared to give my life for whatever it is worth in exchange for his. I have some money and am leaving for the mountains now. I have found someone willing to take me close to where he is and will pray to God that he is still alive.

I ask you pray for Rigo and me. I know that I have been hard on you and not treated you well at times. My heart has not healed properly, nor do I know if it ever will. I have had no guidance in our type of relationship. I have only had misguided expectations no one could ever live up to. To be honest, perhaps I hoped you would fail as a mother and wife so my own failures would not be so apparent when I looked in the mirror. I fight these thoughts every day. I now must face a mother's nightmare. I cannot allow my son to die without an effort to save him. Know that I do this now, so you and the boys will know a husband and father.

Regardless of my fate, understand you deserve happiness and seek it out for the remainder of your days. You must leave the farmhouse in the next three days. It does not belong to me anymore. Follow our "plan" and keep my little boys safe from the rebels. God Bless you and the boys, mi hija! I will send a message by the end of the week to the first location on the map we put together. Please destroy this letter after you read it. I ask and pray you seek some peace in this time of trouble!

America

She took the paper and a clothespin and attached it to the electric wire that ran the length of the kitchen in the old house. She stopped to look at herself in the mirror one final time. "No tears. Fuersa, vieja! Strength, old lady! Use these feeling to help toughen your conviction. It's time to make things right. Take fear and weakness and bury them or they will bury you on this journey. Let God work through you and go claim what the rebels have stolen. If death does find you on this path, then let him find a determined and beautiful America."

CHAPTER TWELVE

Finding Rigo

The trip to the Southern part of the island and Bayamo was a rough, bouncing, eight-hour ride even for the most experienced drivers. This journey proved to be filled with anticipation and contemplation. America chose not to make small talk with Jose nor was she in a state of mind for idle chatter. She found herself wondering what Rigo might be experiencing at that moment. She could only imagine the pain and fear he must be enduring, a physical and emotional hell. She wished she could trade places and would gladly tighten the shackles on her own arms and legs to see him free again. They had to stop more than once to fill the large American Chevrolet with gasoline. The villagers along the way could not be trusted and glared contemptuously at the strangers. No one truly trusted anyone during these last few years. Most Cubans did nothing and were simply pawns waiting to see which side won the war before committing their allegiance to the victor. This was even more evident in the southern part of the island.

In her experience, America knew the villagers stood for nothing of substance, doomed to fall for anything that was cloaked in a veil of hope. Castro filled them with dreams of revolution and a country where everyone would be equal. In truth such a place only existed in the mind. They do not know they were simply trading a tyrant whom they understood as corrupt for another they did not know and could soon fear more than Batista. The promise of a better life was disguised in a military uniform, as many already embraced the vague concept of socialism. They could not see past the promise of security and safety. Yet thinking Cubans knew that whatever name you gave a "savior," the average Cuban would still be left toiling in the sugarcane fields. Living in the heart of poverty was a reality that ran as deep as the ocean that separated Cuba from the United States and the belief that she saved all those who sought her shelter. They would claim loyalty to any country that provided a means to escape poverty.

Internally, no leader has known how to position Cuba to compete and partner with developed nations. They simply continue to allow the whoring of resources and our people. The peasants look within their hunger and can't see beyond tomorrow. She felt sorrow for them but believed that sorrow and self-pity were fuel that propels tyrants into power and the poor into perpetual poverty. Some were born to toil and some were born to be rule. Breaking these patterns takes tenacity and the sacrifices of many. The young were always left to carry this burden of believing that change can lead to opportunity. They often pay for this with their lives, and in the end, what has truly changed?

The setting sun and imminent darkness were a source of desperation for America. She knew the next time the sun rose might be the last day her son breathed. The emotions she was fighting to control were overwhelming. The car moved too slowly on poorly constructed roads. America was afraid they'd break the suspension. Every bump was a potential bullet into Rigo's chance of a life with Juanita and their two children.

America was again tossed airborne after they hit a large pothole. Her head had repeatedly encountered the roof of the car. Everything was moving in slow motion, time was the ever-present enemy. They were approaching Bayamo, and she could see lights glimmering dimly in the distance.

At 9 p.m. the Chevrolet approached the address the rebel informant had scribbled on the piece of paper—Berto Guerra, Casa 13 Bayamo, Calle Norte.

A small row of shacks ran along the edge of the village and past several prominent farms. The disparity between the dilapidated shacks and the main houses on the farms provided a colorful painting of class differences on the island. Each of the shacks were relics that created an image of the affliction of those born into poverty and relegated to its shackles. These former sleeping quarters for impoverished workers during harvest were now permanent homes for their less fortunate residents. The several degrees of separation on the island of Cuba, none more glaring than the political and economic differences between most people and the few powerful and greedy, reflected an ideology that simply redistributed wealth from the middle up and always saved the real economic advantage for those in control. This continued to be true whether control of the government was gained by military force, ideological embezzlement, or both.

America leaned forward in the back seat. "Turn off the lights and slow down as you approach the fifth house on the left. Stop when you get to the tenth."

The car quietly rolled to a stop. "If I'm not back in thirty minutes, go find the police and tell them what happened." America stepped out and walked back the way they'd come. She strained to see a faded number 13 barely legible painted next to the door of the fifth house, which was identical to the others and dark except for the moonlight that served as a backdrop. It looked as if no one was home, at least not awake. Perhaps it wasn't inhabited at all. She prayed the man she needed to see was home. She could feel the pebbles under the soles of her well-worn shoes as she stepped onto the dirt drive that led to the house. Fear swelled within her, and she could feel her heart skipping beats.

She found the wooden door handle weathered, old and brittle. She feared a hard knock on the door might shatter it or prompt the former rebel soldier to fire a barrage of bullets into her heart. Berto Guerra, what an appropriate name for a soldier.

With anticipation and tempered force, America knocked three times and repeated the phrase given to her by the rebel in Havana: "Yo soy la hija de la libertad, ahora buscando justicia y paz (I am the daughter of liberty, now looking for justice and peace)." The rebel supporter turned informant might not even exist. Or he was setting a trap for her.

She stood trembling. Her knuckles were raw from the force of her knock. At first, she heard nothing from inside the hovel. She considered knocking again and reached for the door, when a raspy male voice spoke from the depths of the little rundown shack.

"Quien va ahi?"

America's voice cracked as she recited the rehearsed phrase. "Yo soy la hija de la libertad, ahora buscando justicia y paz."

There was no answer from inside for what seemed like an eternity. She clenched her body, squeezing her arms against her ribs to stop the trembling. A tepid Caribbean breeze blew her hair in front of her face, blocking her view for a split second. At that moment she heard the creaking of the decaying door. A man much older than she'd anticipated peered out at her.

Berto, a short, stout man just over 5 feet tall, looked to be in his 50s. He had an unkempt peppered beard. The smell from either his body or the inside of shack was of musty cigars and rum. An empty left sleeve dangled from his shoulder.

"What do you want, lady?"

"A mutual friend told me you may be able to help me."

"That's a joke, right?" Berto attempted to smile but produced only an eerie smirk. "I have no friends and can't find anything except for my bottle of rum in the dark."

"Please, sir. I need to find my son, Rigoberto Gonzalez, who was captured by the rebels. He was with C Company of the Eighteen Battalion."

Berto looked behind America and moved her aside with his arm. He stared down the road at Jose's taxi. "Is he with you?"

"He drove me here from Havana to meet you."

Berto placed his hand on America's arm and guided her into the house. She glanced back at Jose and nodded, indicating she was not in immediate peril. America walked past the entryway of the one-room dwelling. It had looked much better from the outside.

Berto pointed to a chair by a wooden table stained by the spills from glasses and bottles. The burned edge of the table also served as a cigar holder. No doubt they used their hands to communicate while they drank, as with all Cubans. America didn't move from her spot by door.

"Why come to me, of all people?" Berto asked. "How do I know you're not working with Castro and testing my loyalty?"

"Sir, I came here as a mother and Cuban citizen. I'm simply trying to find my only son who was carried off into the mountains and is to be executed for supporting Batista and our country. Please help me. I'm prepared to pay you."

Berto studied her. He slowly reached over with his one hand and touched what was left of his arm, then quickly pulled it back when he seemed to notice this unconscious movement. He reached instead for the half-filled glass of rum on the table.

"What do you offer me, vieja? I don't know the condition or location of your son. I only know that both the tyrant Batista and now el hijo de puta Castro have shit on me. One steals our country and sells it to the highest bidder, making Cuba a place for greedy evil men to find pleasure. The other lies, kills, and is no less corrupt. His empty lawyer words mean little. He has started stealing too and will steal more once he wins this war. His war has stolen my arm and my dignity and left me to beg for my survival." Berto stared off into nothing.

America chose her next words carefully. She didn't take the old soldier's side but simply addressed the only question he posed. She would need more money to buy Rigo's release. She had 25,000 pesos and five pieces of gold left. She had equally divided the money in the car placing half in the bottom of her shoe and the other half in her waistband pouch. The gold pieces, on her left breast inside her bra, felt uncomfortable but rested directly above her heart.

She took off her shoe and removed the money, now slightly wet from perspiration, and handed it to Berto. "I have twelve thousand pesos if you can take me to where he is. I will die this night if I must but will not leave this earth until I have my son back. If there's only a dead body waiting at the end of this journey, then that's God's will. I won't stop looking for him until the last breath escapes my old tired body. I now beg you, sir, to consider this and help me."

Berto turned his head to the side the way a dog does when trying to understand a human command. "You're a tough vieja. My nephew Pablo Flores was also with his company. I don't know if he survived the attack. He's good man, loyal to his country but confused." He paused. "I'll show you a place in the mountains where they hold prisoners for a short period of time before they're killed. I won't go there with you but can take you to a small opening in the jungle that leads to it. I'll also take your money. I have one condition. If you survive this night and God grants you what you seek, find out if Pablo is alive. I haven't seen him in years but remember him as a good man and soldier."

"Thank you so much, Berto. I will of course see if your nephew's alive if blessed with this opportunity. Can we please leave now? My driver can take us, but I worry the road you speak of may be difficult to reach by car."

"The drive doesn't concern me," Berto said. "But the path from the road to the jail is over a mile and the terrain is tough for a woman of your age." He leaned over and scowled at her. "If you meet these rebels, you must not mention my name, or I promise you that as long as I live, I'll hunt your family down and repay this betrayal many times over. There'll be rebel guards along the trail and they won't be friendly. Your fate may be worse than your son's. I may be sending you straight to your death tonight."

America replaced the shoe she had been holding during their conversation. Berto reached for the money.

"I appreciate the concern, señor. I would gladly die in any way God decides if I can save my son. Your confidence won't be violated, and this money is yours for the kind act of helping me."

Berto took the money and walked towards a closet next to a small wood fireplace that doubled as his kitchen. He opened the door and reached for something. America was frightened as he walked towards her with two items. The pair of shoes under his arm didn't concern her, but the long-bladed knife did. She took a defensive stance and looked towards the door, calculating how to escape.

"Here, woman." He shoved the shoes toward her. "Those shoes you have on will only slow you down in the jungle. This machete may be of use to you too with the bushes or if you're captured. Based on your character, I'm sure you know how to use it. Now let's go before I change my mind."

Berto stopped for a second and walked back to the table to grab the bottle of rum before they left. "I almost forgot my Cuban pain medicine and only amigo." He laughed.

CHAPTER THIRTEEN

The Jungle Jail

The Chevrolet moved slowly over the damp dirt road. It had been over three hours since they'd left Berto's home and was close to 1:00 am. Berto drew small sips from the rum bottle. America was concerned that he'd had too much and would lose some of his faculties. She put on the shoes Berto gave her. She placed the knife inside the elastic part of her underwear and kept the hilt by her hip for fast access. She had spent many hours hacking away at sugarcane during the harvest with a much larger machete but never used one with malicious intent, yet. Jose tried not to show fear, but he sweated constantly and maintained a death grip on the steering wheel.

Shortly after 1:30, Berto signaled Jose to stop. He pointed to an opening on the left side of the road. Next to it was a small fat palm tree that looked out of place amongst the other vegetation.

"Aqui estamos." Berto explained that she was about 1.3 miles from the prison camp. There were several natural obstacles she would have to navigate before she reached the jail. Heading southwest she would encounter a hill about half a mile in. She should not go over but around on the right, the southeastern side. "Stay in the tree line away from the small path. They have a guard there looking for movement on and around the hill." He also spoke of the creek that was directly in front of the prison. "Don't cross in front of the jail. Go around to the west, by a bend in the creek, where the prison guard can't see you. And take off your shoes when you cross so they don't squish and attract the guards' attention."

Jose still held the same death grip on the steering wheel. Berto downed the last bit of rum by tipping the bottom of the bottle towards the sky and leaning his head back. "Mira aqui, anciana. I don't know how this is going to end for you but would not like any more regrets in my life. Just come back to my house and wait until morning to go back to Havana. You don't belong here. This is no game to these people. And you're a woman."

"I appreciate your concern for my life and chastity. I also have experience with regret. I ask one more favor. Do you know anyone with an old car I can use tomorrow? I will be sure to pay them—"

Jose turned to look at her. "I'll be here. From this moment until tomorrow night, I'll be parked wherever you ask. I'll sleep in my car if I must but will wait for your safe return."

America opened the door. "Jose, you've been my angel tonight." She took 2500 pesos and handed it to him. "Do you remember the small airfield we passed less than a mile back? There were three planes there. I have one last favor to ask. Go to the airfield and see if one of the pilots is anywhere nearby. Find out if they're loyal to Batista or to making money. Offer ten thousand pesos for a ride to Jamaica. He must be ready and by his plane in the next three hours and wait until we arrive." Jose bowed his head in affirmation and slowly drove off.

There was a moment of apprehension as she paused and looked back at the car pulling away. She did as she always had. She took the first step and then a second.

She stood for a minute inside the heavily wooded area and got her bearings. The opening was on elevated ground and allowed her to see farther. Once she left the clearing it would be difficult to see more than a few feet in front of her with the foliage and tropical canopy overhead. She replayed the directions in her head.

She headed southwest toward something that might be the hill. She aimed to skirt it on the right. The muddy ground was slippery and difficult to walk on. Thank God she had these shoes.

She froze in panic. A light—no, two—to the left of the hill. Guards smoking a cigarette? Could they see her? She crept forward slowly and kept her head low. She rounded the hill exactly were Berto said to go. The small path seemed barely used, but still she stayed off it and traveled in the woods. The thirty-minute excursion into the jungle and emotional stress of the last few days had worn her down. She was breathing heavily.

As she approached the back of the hill, she saw a dim light ahead and heard trickling water. What if it was an outpost and not the jail? She inched forward step by step until she could see the creek. It was about three times bigger than she was expecting, probably swollen by the recent heavy rains. It must have been twenty feet across.

She pushed aside her fear and doubt and took her shoes off, holding them in one hand as she traversed the creek trying not to make too much noise. It was deeper than she'd expected, up to her waist and extremely cold.

There it was. She could see the building, but with a fence around it. Berto hadn't said anything about a fence. There must be an opening. She peeked over the edge of the embankment for a gate or some means inside. She saw it—right behind a guard with a very large rifle.

America lay on her stomach. How would she get past that guard? How the hell did she get this far? What if Rigo wasn't there? So many thoughts came to her in waves. It all would come down to the next decision she made. So much rested on her pushing through the doubt, the exhaustion, and the uncertainty of her actions. But most of all her fear.

Could she possibly surprise the guard and use the machete to silence him? What if there were more rebels inside? America squinted for a better view of the structure and the guard. She could make out his position, sitting with his rifle on his lap. Charging the man with the machete would not be a wise move. She must use some level of intelligence here to outsmart him. She could debate this with herself all night, but she couldn't wait any longer. *Dios, if you are present, please have mercy on my soul! If you must take one life tonight, let it be mine and not my son's. I am prepared to die tonight if you grace this old woman with a long life for her only born son, amen.*

America placed the machete in front of her on dry level ground. She made the sign of the cross, pushed her hands into the soft and slick clay, and lifted her body erect. She replaced the machete in her waistband. The blade wasn't visible and hung in a vertical position on her back with the tip almost reaching the back of her knee. She took a deep breath and held her hands at breast level. She did the only thing she could, moved forward.

CHAPTER FOURTEEN

The Price of a Life

"Nobody ever did, or ever will, escape the consequences of his choices."

-Alfred A. Montapert

Her steps were slow and calculated. She looked only in front of her as she waited for the guard to discover her presence. The distance between her and her fate was slowly closing. She was fifty yards from the guard when he jumped to his feet and lifted the barrel of his weapon. "Alto! Who goes there?"

Fear and adrenaline fused together and her heart was racing faster than she could remember. She raised her head. "Viva Fidel! Es una vieja del pueblo, an old lady from town. I slipped into the damn creek and am completely lost and frozen. Please help me find my way back home."

"Don't move or I'll shoot you where you stand! What do you mean, lost?"

"I was supposed to meet my boyfriend out here away from his wife. The lying bastard didn't make it. This is the story of my life."

The guard lowered his rifle a little and seemed to be studying her body. "Walk slowly or die." He pointed to the side of the building away from the door. She came close enough to see the building was constructed of stone. She could feel the blade against her buttocks, making small cuts in her skin with every step. Blood was dripping slowly down the back of her thigh. She bit her lower lip and kept walking. The guard began to walk toward her, the rifle aimed squarely at her chest. He did not take his eyes off her.

"So, you came to meet a lover, eh?" The soldier was eyeing her. "You're one lucky lady. You met me, Alian." They were only ten steps from each other. "Stop there and raise your hands over your head."

America did as ordered, praying her machete wouldn't slip out of her waistband. He looked her over for a minute and seemed to like what he saw. He had a weathered face darkened partly by the tropical sunshine, but mostly because of the life he'd led. He inched closer and began to morph into a menacing character. She knew she had only one choice.

How would she do it? Should she wait until he was close enough to touch? Yes, this was the only way she could pull the machete out and plunge it deep into this man. He was of no consequence to her. He couldn't be, or she wouldn't have the heart to do what she must. The guard was five steps away. Close enough that she could smell his breath and see that he was also breathing heavily. The smell of cigar smoke and alcohol permeated the air around him. She would have to wait until he was directly in front of her and lowered the rifle. Three feet away. He stopped walking. Again he looked at her like a predator about to leap.

"Calm down, my new amigo," America said. "You can see I have no weapon and I'm alone. I know what it's like to be lonely."

He paused and seemed to relax slightly. "You're too old to be a whore. If you were selling something, you'd be a lot skinnier. No problema. Keep moving around the building."

America began to panic. He still wasn't close enough. He'd certainly shoot her before she had enough time. "I'm not a whore, simply a woman who needs to be loved by a real man upon occasion. But my clothes are wet and I need my hands to take them off. Unless you'd like to help?"

Still, the old soldier didn't approach. He glanced back at the front door where his chair now sat vacant. He looked away and scanned the surrounding woods. "All right, lady. You'll get what you came for. Keep your hands up."

He relaxed his hold on the weapon and took small steps towards her. She could clearly see the opening of the muzzle as he rested it on her left breast, touching the pieces of gold that she'd stored in her bra. The guard didn't notice the coins against her breasts, took the last step towards her, but left the rifle in the same location. His odor was filthier as he closed the gap between them. Holding his finger over the trigger, he grabbed the back of her head with his other hand, wrapped his fingers around her neck, and squeezed.

She knew that death would be her fate in the next few seconds, either by a bullet or by the hands of this angry little man. The guard pulled her closer to him, close enough to kiss her. He paused short of her lips, deeply inhaled her scent, and smiled. "This is a smell I haven't had for months."

It was time. She smiled back at the horrid man who stood between her and her son and began to count backwards. *Three, two, one.* Her hand went quickly to the machete handle. She pulled it out sideways and, with her free hand, pushed the rifle muzzle away from her chest. The guard's eyes widened. America drew the blade back and lunged at the guard. She felt the tip of the large knife touch the guard just before he smashed her face with the butt of his weapon. Everything went blurry and she hit the ground.

America shook her head. The guard was lying on top of her. The smell of his rage surpassed the stench of his breath. She could barely make out the machete behind the guard, where he'd apparently thrown it. His hands gripped her throat and began to squeeze. She felt herself drifting away, her mind filled with happy memories. She went back to Enrique, he was in her arms, courting her and telling her how beautiful their life would be. Her mind flashed to Rigo as a boy playing in the fields, and he would hug her for no reason. Juanita and the boys. She was a great mother. Her patience in explaining things to her small children surpassed the support America had given her own son. The drifting was interrupted by cursing and yelling near her ear.

"You stupid damn whore! Did you really think you could kill me? I'm a soldier, and I've taken many lives already. Tonight, yours will be added to the list. Before you die, witch, you'll feel real pain. Not the gentle lovemaking of your limp boyfriend but something that will leave a permanent scar on your dead body."

America let herself drift away again. The choking hand of the guard was slowly leading her to another world. She was ready.

"Soon, Rigo, I pray we meet and I can be a better mother to you in this next life." The guard, still violently spewing curses at her and showering her with his spittle, reached down to unzip his pants.

America began to regain consciousness. The guard was no longer on top of her. She coughed and reached for throat. Her assailant lay next to her with the machete blade in his back. The tip protruded from his chest, preventing his torso from lying flat on the ground. Behind the dead rebel were two forms. One stood thirty feet away while the other was at the feet of the guard, one arm at his side and the other missing. Berto! Jose approached behind him.

A few more seconds passed as she continued coughing and tried to breathe normally. She attempted to speak but the words did not come. She put her hand around her throat and struggled. The words came out slowly and raspy. "Gracias, Berto, gracias."

"So, you're alive old woman? Get up. They'll be changing guards soon." With one foot on the corpse's back, he slid the blade free and wiped the blood off onto the guard's shirt. "My favorite knife, I'm happy to see it again." He grinned and reached down to help America up. "Let's go, Let's go."

America stumbled forward but did not follow the men instead she headed toward the building. Berto shoved the machete under his belt and picked up the AK 47 leaning against the building. "Damn it," he whispered. "I knew this woman was going to get me killed in this goddamn jungle." He followed her towards the door.

CHAPTER FIFTEEN

Darkness Always Precedes the Light

It was 5:30 in the morning, just a little over an hour before the sun would begin its journey across the island and illuminate the recently hidden landscape. The tops of the tall trees were the first to signal its arrival. Some saw the light as hope and inspiration. Others were thankful for another day and the opportunity to pursue their hopes and dreams. But some cursed the light, for it revealed the darkness within them.

The wooden door was secured with a Master padlock. America pulled at it, but it didn't budge. Berto turned his shoulder toward the door and together they both pushed. Several attempts later the door was as secure as when they first crashed into it. On the fifth try, they paused and looked towards the creek. It was faint, but they could both see a handful of small flickering lights moving towards them. Sweat beaded on their faces despite the cool morning breeze. Jose approached them.

"Help us here, hombre," Berto said.

Jose reached out his fist and opened it to reveal a key. "Maybe this'll help. It was in the guard's pocket."

Berto grabbed the key as America lifted the lock. He rammed the key into the hole and twisted. The familiar sound of a snap releasing its grip followed.

America quickly took the lock off and prayed there would be no other obstacle. She grabbed the handle of the door and swung it open. The men did not follow her inside.

Little moonlight came in through the barred windows, making it difficult to see. She could however hear the buzzing, constant and loud. The flies swarmed around her. The smell in the room gagged her, feces and ammonia, and another, worse smell: rotting flesh. All her fears resurfaced. She stumbled to the back of the room and into a hallway. "Rigo, Rigo!" She didn't get a response.

With the next step, she tripped over something and hit the ground. She reached out and felt what she thought might be a leg. She subdued a scream. The outline of a body became visible. She leaned towards it and could see the entry wound in the back of the man's head as well as the uniform of a Batista soldier. What a cowardly way to kill a man.

Suddenly she was gripped with a gut-wrenching fear. "Oh my God! Rigo?" She had no way to know unless she looked at his face. She reached over with both arms and flipped the body towards her. She felt wet blood and chunks of flesh and brain. She forced herself to look closer.

The shock of seeing a face so completely disfigured felt like a violation of human dignity. At the sight of what was left of his face, her hand instantly covered her mouth—hands covered with blood, some of which trickled into her mouth. She spat several times, then examined the dead soldier in front of her. He no longer had a forehead. She touched his chin and gently turned his head to the side.

"Aye, Dios mio, gracias." It was not Rigo. She quickly turned around and began to crawl, still calling out for her son.

Someone said, "Rigo." Her heart began to race and she increased the speed of her crawl. Once again she heard the muffled sound. "Rigo." A few more paces brought her to a man lying on his stomach by the wall.

As she reached the man, he looked over his shoulder at her. "Who are you and what in the name of all the saints are you doing in this hell?"

"My name is America Gonzalez. I'm looking for my son, Lieutenant Rigoberto Gonzalez, from Company C of the Eighteen Battalion." He was a large man with broad shoulders. His face was beaten badly and one eye was swollen shut. His hands were bound in chains and connected to a metal loop cemented into the floor. She wasn't sure, but he almost appeared to be grinning at her.

"This must be another hallucination."

She placed one hand on his collar and spoke in a whisper. "I am who I say I am, please tell me if my son is here."

The solder's eyes opened wider. "Holy shit. This is really happening. I'm Sergeant Flores, I served with your son."

The room began to slowly spin. "Served?" Past tense. It could only mean... She wanted to stop listening to him but had to know what happened.

"Vamonos, vieja!" Berto yelled from the door. "We won't make it out of here alive if we don't leave now."

America returned her gaze to Flores who paused at hearing the voice outside of the building. "America, I don't know if he's alive, but he's here. They blindfold us during the day and either beat us or shoot us if we dare speak to each other. I haven't seen him, but I know he was brought here with me when they captured us in the camp. The officers are at the other end of the building."

She lifted herself to her feet, extended her hands in case she stumbled again, and walked towards the back of the building, every step accompanied with a raspy "Rigo." She felt like a creature or ghost reaching for its victims.

After several steps she heard from the right, "Sigue adelante, keep going." From the left she heard several voices. "No soy, not me," some said. She could make out a few other men in the same position as Sergeant Flores, tied up and in chains. There were six so far and she was almost to the end of the building. Her anxiety grew.

And then she heard it. "Mima?" That voice, that sweet voice, it could only be one person.

"Mi hijo, si, es tu mama." She dropped to the ground and crawled to her son. Relief flooded her body. He was sitting on the floor pulling on his chains. "Mi hijo, mi hijo." She collapsed on him and wrapped her arms around his shoulders. With both hands chained he could only rest his head on her shoulder.

America grabbed his face with both hands. "How the hell do I get you out of here? We have no time to waste. How do we break these chains?"

Rigo, beaten and close to starvation, looked down at his wrists. "Mima, you have done more than any son could imagine. Go! I can face this but to know that you'll join me is too much to bear. Now go!"

America hugged him and kissed his cheek, smearing it with what resembled dark red lipstick. She pushed herself up and sprinted to the door.

CHAPTER SIXTEEN

A Beautiful Skeleton

She sidestepped the body by the front door. Jose and Berto were ready to run towards the creek. America ran past the two men but not to the creek. She sped to the dead guard, knelt over his body, flipped it over, and began to search.

"Hijo de tu madre, you must have another key. I will kill you twice…" She went through every pants pocket and his shirt. Jose and Berto took a few steps towards the creek. The lights were closer. Nothing in the outside pockets. His face looked sad and pathetic. What if this man had just stayed home with his family?

America ripped open his shirt and felt the material inside. She could not escape the red blood on the green fatigues but at this point she was immune to it. She cursed the man silently. Then she felt something in the inside flap of his pocket. She groped for the opening of the flap and stuck her hand inside. There it was, a key! An old-fashioned skeleton key.

She ran to the door, where Berto stepped in front of her. "We must leave now, vieja. They'll kill me on sight."

"Go, go! I have to try and save him. If this doesn't work I'll die next to him."

Berto turned to go. "If we make it to the opening where you came in, the car's hidden behind a row of palm trees across the road. Do you know how to use this?" He leaned the guard's gun against a tree. Jose stood behind him rocking back and forth in obvious panic.

This time she leapt over the dead body, almost slipping as she landed. Rigo was in the same position with his hands covering his face. She jumped towards him and without a word grabbed the lock restraining him. Her hands where shaking so badly that she missed the hole on the first attempt. She found her mark on the second try. As she turned the key, for the second time this evening she heard the beautiful click. The lock opened. She could see Rigo's bewilderment and confusion. He embraced his mother.

"Vamonos, mi hijo. The rebels are almost here." She helped Rigo to his feet. He could not walk at first. Under the tears in his uniform she could see open wounds. She placed his arm over her neck and shoulder and began their journey across the building. Some of the other prisoners called to them. "Who is it? Did you find him?"

Once they reached the door, the smell of the jungle hit Rigo in the face. It couldn't be confused with any other. He stopped and gently turned his mother to face him and held both of her hands. He then opened her hand and removed the skeleton key.

"Mima, you have to go now. I'll be right behind you but can't leave these men here to die. I need to know that you're away from here before the other rebels arrive. Don't argue with me."

America looked sadly at him but knew time was fleeting. She pointed to the opening across the creek. "I'll be waiting for you there." She then pointed to the tree where the rifle was resting. They both looked behind the building, across the creek towards the lights. Only three of them, thank God, and coming from the opposite direction of their retreat.

Rigo turned around and started to head back into the nightmare that kept him trapped for days.

"Rigo, there's a Sergeant Flores in there who knows you. He gave me hope you were still alive."

He went inside, past the smell, past the flies, and past the dead soldier. Six soldiers were left inside. He unlocked the first lock. He didn't know the man but saw he could walk. The second man wasn't moving. Rigo touched his neck. The cold and clammy skin led him to believe the man was no longer alive, and the lack of a pulse confirmed it. The third prisoner was close to the wall and seemed unable to turn around. Rigo didn't need to see his face. The size of his body and shoulders identified him. Rigo reached for the lock. The soldier turned his head.

"Lieutenant, is this really happening? Are we getting out of here, sir?"

"If we hurry, Flores. There are three other men to release and more rebels will be here in minutes."

"Where's your mother? My God, how did she find us and free you?"

Rigo opened the lock and turned to free the next man, but before he took a step, Sergeant Flores grabbed him by his collar.

"No sir, I'll do that. You go get your mother to safety. I'll take care of these men."

Flores reached for the window ledge above him and pulled himself to his feet. The bullet hole in his thigh had turned greenish black, indicating gangrene. Flores extended his hand for the key as he took a step toward the other chained men. Rigo clenched his fist.

"Su mama, Rigo. Take care of your mother first."

"Damn it, Flores." Rigo slapped the key into Flores's hand. "There's a rifle leaning against the tree outside. The rebels are coming across the creek from the east, to the right as you step outside. I'll be headed west to find my mother. Flores, it's best we split up. We'll have a better chance of making it out of here."

Flores had already limped his way to the next soldier. Rigo walked outside and pulled the dead guard out of view from the oncoming rebels. His next steps were to the creek. His legs were still numb from lying down on the hard dirt floor and constant beatings during the interrogations. As he reached the creek, over the sound of the flowing water he started to hear the distant voices of the approaching rebels. No doubt some of the same men that had beat him daily and threatened to kill everyone in his family.

The beatings had grown more violent with every occurrence. On the first day of his capture they cut the nametag and rank from his uniform. The rebel who had dragged him into the jail began the torture. He held the large knife in front of the hole where his nametag had been and began to cut at his chest. Rigo could still hear the long-bearded man talking as he was slicing open his chest. "Today I'll have to take your heart out. I don't really like cutting the heart as it bleeds so much. If you don't tell me the plans for this southern aggression against the peaceful farmers and protectors of freedom, I'll have to clean up later." With every sentence, the rebel would plunge the knife deeper into his skin.

Rigo was sure he was going to die in this most heinous fashion yet did not speak except for stating his name and rank. The pain at times didn't allow him to complete his full name without pausing and grunting as the blade went deeper into his chest. At one point he believed that the knife had pierced his heart and prepared to die. It might have been easier if he had, but instead he willed himself to live, not for himself, but for Juanita and the boys. For three days they beat and tortured him. He could tolerate the pain most of the time. It was more difficult when he saw a soldier executed. And then another. They left the bodies inside overnight so the smell and reality of death saturated their thoughts.

Once he reached the tree line on the opposite side of the creek he could see the opening where America told him she would be. As he headed towards it, he did something he hadn't done in a long time. He started to pray, not for himself but for the five men that remained behind. "Mi padre, please help" were the only words he was able to utter before he heard gunfire from the building, one after the other, three in total. Rigo turned back to help the men but was stopped by a raspy voice.

"Mi hijo, I'm here, let's hurry." Rigo looked at his mother in the moonlight and had never seen her so beaten. Her voice had not returned completely. She had tried to wash away some of the blood in the creek but the stains that remained blotched her face. He needed to help her out of the jungle. Or was it America who needed to help him out? She extended her hand to him and after he looked back one last time towards the jail, he returned the gesture and grabbed her hand.

CHAPTER SEVENTEEN

A Field of Dreams?

They walked briskly away and could only hope all remaining soldiers also made it out alive.

"Mima, how are Juanita and the boys?" They spoke in whispers.

"Juanita knows she must leave the farm and village. We made a plan and have several houses she can stay in for a short time. She knows if you made it out alive rebels wouldn't stop until we were all captured and dead."

"She doesn't deserve this worry and pain." He paused for a moment. "Mima, how did you find me? How did you do what the Cuban Army couldn't do?" America continued to lead the way, the old woman on point in the jungle and the veteran soldier following. She pointed to the side of the ridge they must take.

"Mi hijo, this is no time for talk."

Rigo knew deep inside he'd made the best decision for his family. Each one of them would have done the same. Three shots? There were five of them still there. Certainly they would have shot more than once at each of the five men, especially since they had a weapon. Flores, however, was by far the best shot in the company. Was it possible that he simply positioned himself somewhere and took out the approaching rebels? This was the way he wanted to believe it all played out.

Once they reached the opening that led to the road, America looked towards the left. Rigo pulled back a large palm leaf that covered the opening. He couldn't help but notice a large black Chevrolet backing out of the jungle and about to head down the road—away from where they are standing. America looked at Rigo plainly panicked about losing their getaway car.

He knew yelling would draw unwanted attention. The area had many Castro supporters who would love to show their loyalty by turning in an escaped Cuban soldier. Rigo looked around and found a rock. He stepped out onto the road hurled the rock with the arm of a seasoned centerfielder. The rock smashed into the roof of the car, and a scream came from inside.

"Oh my God, we're dead! They found us!"

A deeper voice yelled, "Stop, viejo! You think the rebels have run out of bullets and now throw rocks?" The car came to a halt.

Rigo limped towards the paused car and opened the back door and helped his mother inside. He quickly joined her. Before the door was even closed, the driver floored the gas.

"Did you find someone, Jose?" America said. "At the airfield?"

The driver did not or could not respond. Rigo remembered Jose, who had helped on the farms for many years, and was now sizing up the man in the passenger seat.

"Gracias, Jose. This must be difficult for you." Rigo knew talking to people was a good way to calm them down. "I appreciate you helping my mother and me, with all my heart. One day I may get a chance to repay you."

The other man looked at Jose, waited a moment, then turned to America. "There's one pilot who has a home next to the small airfield. He agreed to take your son to Montego Bay. He may still be waiting. As we were leaving I heard his shortwave radio, rebels checking in with each guard area. I'm not sure we can trust this man."

"Excuse me, my new friend," Rigo said, "but I don't know you. Why are you talking to my mother about Montego Bay?"

The man didn't answer.

"Rigo, Berto saved my life tonight. He also told me about the jail. Oh my God Berto! Your nephew Pablo was in the jail as well."

Berto glared at America, Rigo glared at Berto. Jose sat up straighter and moved his body to the edge of the seat as he gripped the steering wheel even tighter.

"You're Sergeant Flores's uncle? The rebel sympathizer who fought against us? What is this, what's going on here? I should kill you now myself."

Berto calmly looked at Rigo and placed his hand on the grip of his old companion, the machete. "I have been many things to many people, but today I'm the man who saved you and your mother from certain death."

America put her hand on top of Rigo's. "I was almost raped and killed by that guard outside of the jail. This man saved me. He also hates Castro as much as we do."

Rigo noticed Berto's missing arm. Of course he hates Castro. Once the peasants were of no more use to him, he simply sent them back to their villages regardless of their injuries. "If you helped my mother, then I'm in your debt. I've had a difficult few days and must thank you for what you've done."

"I'm so sorry, Berto. I should have told you he was in there."

"Please tell me, was he alive?" Berto seemed almost afraid to ask. "I haven't seen him in a long time, but he was a good man."

Before America could respond, Rigo looked directly at the one-armed passenger. "He's a great man and soldier. I'm very proud of Sergeant Flores. He saved our asses more than once. He was very alive when I left. He insisted on releasing the others after I freed him. He pleaded with me to get my mother to safety. I took the chains off his wrists and left the AK-47 with him. If I know Sergeant Flores, he'll get those men out of there and take a few rebels with him in the process."

Berto let out a long breath and relaxed in the seat. "It's now in God's hands. There'll be a company of Castro's men looking for payback and wanting to kill anyone in the area. I'm afraid the farmers and workers are sure to get some unwanted attention."

As they pulled in to the airfield, there were no planes on the field. Was this a setup?

"Vamonos! Let's get out of here now," Rigo and Berto said at the same time.

Jose didn't move. He sat with both hands firmly planted on the wheel at the ten and two positions. He leaned forward again, this time squinting. He pointed to a hangar about a hundred yards away. A man stepped out from it. "Berto, that looks like the guy. Yes, it is, and he's waving at us."

No one spoke or moved for several seconds. Rigo and Berto stared at each other for what seemed like an eternity.

"Rigo, I don't think there're rebels in there," Berto said. "They would've ambushed us at the entrance of the airfield. They're guerrillas and use the jungle to their advantage. I can't see them hiding out bunched up in a hangar."

The man had a point. Rebels surround a target. Hiding in a building didn't make sense. "You may be right about this," Rigo said. "Jose, move up toward the hangar, slowly. If the man makes any sudden moves or you see someone else in there, drive away faster than you've driven in your life."

The large sedan got closer to the hangar but stopped a hundred feet short. Jose cranked down the window but only a few inches, as if it would serve as protection against a barrage of gunfire.

The pilot jogged over to the car. "You made it. I wasn't sure I'd ever see you men again. I put the plane in the hangar after I heard on my radio that some men had escaped a Castro jail. Some weeks back I accidently found their communication frequency in this area. If I hear there's trouble, I can take to the sky and find a safe place to put my plane down. Those bastards have tried to take it from me several times already and have even shot at me. We gotta go now if we're going to make it to Jamaica. Word on the streets is that Batista is beginning to lose support of the military and some of his generals are refusing to fight the rebels."

The man looked in the back seat and saw America and Rigo for the first time. His eyes widened. "Which one of you is flying with me?"

At the exact same time, Rigo and America pointed to each other. Rigo reached over, opened his mother's door, and pointed to the plane now visible through the crack in the hangar.

"Mima, go now. I'll find Juanita and the boys and make plans to leave the island. I know many people in Havana would love to see us all back in a Castro jail. I'll be careful."

America listened to her son speak but didn't respond. She first turned to the open door, grabbed the handle, and pulled it shut. "You tell me to get on a plane and leave? Do you hear yourself? They want you dead! They'll care less about an old lady. If you love your family and respect your mother, then get your stubborn Cuban ass onto that plane, now! I'll find Juanita and make plans to get her to the United States. You know this is the best way."

Rigo had learned to fight through his real feelings regardless of his circumstances, whether it was never knowing his father or seeing people he cared for die in front of him. Yet now he was choked up in a car with strangers, his mother beaten down from saving him. He reached over for her hand and began to cry. These were old tears, tears that had never been released. He cried with complete abandon and disregard for who was watching. It was what some call an ugly cry but one that was cathartic. It was a liberation unlike what he had just experienced in jail, a complete emotional release.

"Vamonos, por favor," the pilot said. "We must leave or I won't be cleared for this trip. Now, either one of you."

America wiped away her son's tears, kissed his cheek, then opened his door. "I'll see you again soon."

Rigo returned her kiss and stepped out of the car. He looked back to Jose and Berto. "Please take care of her and make sure she gets to Pinal Del Rio safely." America reached into her blouse, produced five pieces of gold, and handed them to her son.

Rigo and the pilot raced to the plane. Rigo jumped in, and the pilot thrust the propeller towards the ground. The propeller hesitated, sputtered, then roared under its own power. The pilot swung open the second hangar door and climbed into the front seat of the airplane. They taxied to the runway and within a minute took flight into the cloudless sky, going higher and higher as the plane passed the surrounding mountains and disappeared in the horizon.

CHAPTER EIGHTEEN

Left Behind – Juanita's Story

Juanita walked into the farmhouse completely drained from traveling to Havana with the boys. Once again the day proved fruitless. The Cuban government and army had no damn idea what the hell they were doing. It had been over a month and no word on Rigo. The gossip in town was that Castro was winning and capturing Cuban soldiers all over the island. There was talk of Rigo being captured. These townspeople talked too much and loved to put fear into everyone's heart. Certainly they would have contacted her some way? A letter or an officer would have brought news if something bad had happened. Yet nothing.

The officer at the base yesterday said the same thing she'd heard every day when she traveled from Pinal Del Rio to Havana. "Nothing to report, ma'am." She could tell that there was indeed something to report. Today had been different. There were fewer men on base. She heard them yelling at each other. It was so chaotic they wouldn't even let her on the base. "Sorry, ma'am, but we have a situation to take care of."

"A situation? What the hell does that mean? I have a situation too—I don't know where my husband is."

"Sorry, but you'll have to leave or we'll need to restrain you."

Juanita looked down at Francisco and Carlos and then back at the guard. "What the hell are you talking to me about? I'm a citizen with a husband who's an officer in the Cuban Army. I have my two little boys with me, and you talk of restraining?"

The guard looked down at Francisco and Carlos. "I'm sorry, I'm simply following orders." He glanced at the other two soldiers in the guard shack then lowered his voice. "Many others are also looking for information on their husbands. The truth is, we don't know. A lot has happened in the last few days, we've lost contact with some of the units in the south... I've said too much already. Please go now and come back another time."

The young soldier looked like he was fifteen years old and more scared than he let on. Juanita took the boys' hands and walked away.

When Juanita returned from Havana she took a brief look around the farmhouse to see if America was home. The boys were hungry and complained all the way back on the bus. Traveling with children was never fun.

She didn't find America and went to the refrigerator to get something to feed the boys. She always thought the refrigerator was a luxurious status symbol above her means. America bought the Coldspot from a catalog and had it delivered to the island a few years ago. Juanita didn't think there was anything wrong with the old ice chest that everyone in Cuba grew up with. It was nice to greet the iceman every other day. It was simple and personal. This machine did look nice and fancy, but a waste, just more for the townspeople to talk about. "Look at America, she's doing so well," they would say to her. What they meant was, "Oh, more nice things this lady has bought because of the gambler. I wonder who lost their money to pay for the contraption."

She'd heard the talk since the first time she went out with Rigo. She hated all the small-town gossip and on some occasions wished she were back working in the fields with her parents. Back there, life was simple. They worked hard and enjoyed each other's company. There was no worry of anyone saying anything bad about her family. They had nothing and labored hard to earn a living like everyone else. It was different here in Pinal Del Rio.

As she approached the refrigerator she could see the old clothespin on the wire and the letter beneath it. It was her and America's way of communicating with each other when they had to leave. There had been many letters left on clothespins that spoke of dinners to be cooked and chores that needed to be done.

Juanita did not take it down and read it right away. She opened the refrigerator and looked for some ham and bread for the boys. The machine made a constant hissing sound when it was plugged into the wall. It reminded her of a swarm of bees and was rather annoying. The boys shoveled down the sandwiches and milk. As she watched them, she knew her place was here, in this house, taking care of these beautiful boys.

Juanita grabbed the letter, laid it on the table and sat down to read. The boys started yelling and pushing each other by the sink.

"No, you do it. I did it last time and you never helped me." The boys were arguing, again, over whose turn it was to wash the plates. Juanita walked over to the boys and went down to one knee to be at eye level with the little men.

"Que pasa mis niños?" Juanita always tried to be calm when talking to her boys. "Why the yelling?" She gave the boys a chance to share their thoughts and feelings on the subject. When they became locked in a staring contest, she was tickled at how these two little people communicated. They were most definitely Rigo's children—handsome but stubborn.

"Let me have both of your eyes and full attention," Juanita said. "You two are brothers, and brothers need to work together. There will be times when all you have is each other and no one else to rely on. Carlito, do you love your brother?"

Carlito looked at the floor. "Yes, but I don't like it when he's mean to me."

"Francisco, do love your brother?"

The older brother appeared to be shooting laser beams through his eyes at the younger. "I do, but he makes me so mad sometimes. He does it on purpose!"

"Francisco, don't give your power away to anyone, ever. When you lose your temper, you let other people control you, and they'll often take advantage of it. Your little brother needs your help with the dishes. Let's think of a way you can work together. Is there anything here that maybe can help you reach the sink, Carlito? What about you, Francisco, do you see anything that can help your brother?" Juniata scanned the room and stopped her gaze at the milk crate by the door. After a few seconds passed, Francisco pointed at it.

"The milk crate! He can step on it and reach the sink." The boys raced each other to the crate and brought it back to the sink. Francisco carefully helped his brother onto the crate and began to instruct him on the best way to clean the dishes. Juanita returned to her chair at the table, opened the letter, and began to read. *Mi Nina, I doubt you have had any success . . ."*

CHAPTER NINTEEN

The Bookends of Fear and Despair

"We draw our strength from the very despair in which we have been forced to live. We shall endure."

-Cesar Chavez

The words from the letter drained Juanita completely, and she slumped down in her chair. She raised her hand to her forehead as if checking her temperature. She then lowered her hand and covered her mouth.

"No, Dios mio. This can't be true. This cannot be his fate." Juanita looked up and saw the boys standing next to her and staring. Francisco was holding his mother's free hand and Carlos was holding onto her leg. Juanita looked at the boys and then at the letter. She tried to understand what this meant and what she should do next.

Oh my God, we have to leave. The plan America mentioned in the letter included a succession of four safe houses and people America believed she could trust. Juanita and the boys were to stay at each of them no longer than five days. They had made the plan several weeks ago when it seemed the war might shift towards a Castro victory and the rebels would be looking for the families of the Batista soldiers who fought against them. This meant no one in the village could be trusted. The wavering locals would surely shift their support to Castro and be more than happy to turn them in as enemies of the Revolution.

When they'd first talked about it, Juanita believed it was just America being dramatic. There was no way it would ever be needed. It now realistically appeared all may be lost including the love of her life. Her head started spinning when she stood up. Nausea took over her body. The thought of him in a jail was too much to bear. The thought of him being dead was a dagger in her heart. She reread the words and searched for hope and strength in some part of them.

"They have him," America's letter said. But he was resilient. A strong man. He'd be able to hold out until they saw he was just doing his job as a soldier. Then they would free him. Yes, this could happen. If he kept his cool and didn't let his emotions get the best of him. As soon as this thought entered her mind, she realized he wasn't one to back down or give in to anyone. Juanita prayed he did not expose this side of him. They'd kill him for sure.

My God, America is going after him. Juanita was stunned. What did that mean or look like? How can an aging woman find a prisoner in an enemy camp? Let alone help him escape? She was, however, the toughest person she'd ever met.

Juanita pulled herself together and stood up straight, posture erect and disposition firm. She took the boys by the hands and led them to the bedroom. She reached under the bed and pulled out a large leather suitcase.

"Alright, my little busy bees, we're going on an adventure."

Juanita had the suitcase completely stuffed with what she considered their most important belongings. This was a difficult task. What do you take with you of value that cannot be replaced? How many people on the island would be in this same position soon? One suitcase per household to transport possessions accumulated throughout a lifetime. She unconsciously began to shed tears as she picked up a beautiful glass frame given to them for their wedding but knew it was too heavy to carry. Inside was a picture of her and Rigo in his military uniform. They were so happy in that picture. It was before any real threat of a war or revolution. It was a time where planning their future and raising children filled their conversations. The frame was not the true thing of value. But the photo was a symbol, a glimpse of a special moment shared by two people who loved one another. The expensive frame would need to stay back on the farm. She wondered what photo and memory would be placed in it next.

The suitcase was full of essential items for the children. It was heavier than she imagined. Rigo had always carried it for her. Now she knew how heavy it had been for him. She placed the remaining household items in three boxes. On the boxes she wrote, "Please save these for us somewhere so when our family returns we will have these few items to remind us of our time on the farm together – Juana Maria Gonzalez." She didn't know when that would be, or if ever.

Juanita struggled to lift the suitcase but was able to maneuver it to the front porch. She needed to get them all safely to the first house on the list. Normally if she had something heavy to carry she would ask Jose, their farm helper, to give her a ride, but his sedan wasn't on the property. He must be on an errand of some kind.

The first house on the list was committed to her memory. She knew this family and they'd attended her wedding. Carmela Perez was about the same age as America, and her house was about a mile northwest of Pinal Del Rio in Las Ovas. There was no way she could make that trip by foot carrying the suitcase. She at least needed to make it to town to find a taxi.

She began the walk with the boys and the heavy luggage. She could only carry it for several yards before she needed to rest. Carlos and Francisco tried to help, Francisco holding up the rear of the suitcase and Carlos the front. Francisco would make grunting noises with every very short leg of the 30-minute trip to show he was giving it his full effort. Carlos would attempt to hold the front of the suitcase with one hand and walk backwards, slowing them down more than helping. He did however look back at his mother every few steps to gain her approval and make sure she was observing his deed of chivalry and strength. The extra burden of the weight was worth seeing the smile on his face.

Once they made it to edge of town she saw several cars across from the general store and barbershop about a block away. There were also soldiers everywhere. She had never seen so many armed soldiers on the streets of any city. They didn't seem to be searching for anyone or anything. They were simply gathered on every corner almost as if waiting for something to happen.

"Wait here, boys. I'll go find a taxi." Carlos and Francisco sat down on top of the suitcase.

Juanita didn't want to ask anyone she recognized for a ride. The driver at the end of the taxi line was a stranger and, like many of the other taxi drivers in Cuba, in his fifties. He needed Juanita to help lift and shove the suitcase into the trunk of the old Buick. She did not remember the address of any of the safe houses but only remembered how to get there.

When they arrived at the house she worried she wouldn't be welcomed, especially with the panic going around the island about Castro and the revolution. They stepped out of the car and left the suitcase on the side of the dirt road by the mailbox. The small house had an odd shape and, like many Cuban houses, stood on stilts about three feet above the ground to avoid flooding during hurricane season. Behind the house, sugarcane stalks ranged as far as the eye could see. Sugarcane became a national symbol for the island and boomed in the mid to late 1800s. Steam locomotives were introduced to Cuba, making it only the seventh country in the world and first in Latin America to have a railroad system. Shortly afterwards, individual farms began being replaced by large privately owned sugarcane mills.

Carmela's farm was small in comparison, and her only means of income was selling cane at whatever price was established by the large international companies that controlled the market. Frequently she would only make enough during the harvest period or Zafra, as it was known across the Caribbean, to pay her workers, plant the next crop, and live off the small amount remaining. The Zafra lasted from January through May. Many Cubans had to survive the remainder of the year on the paltry amount of money made during harvest. The situation was the same for every small farmer in the country. They barely made it from year to year and were at the mercy of the larger, mostly American-owned corporations that dominated the market. Castro had appealed to these workers who wanted change and a livable wage. Many believed that any economic situation would be better than their current one.

Before Juanita and the children reached the front door, Carmela greeted her on the porch. She stepped out of the house with arms wide open and a stalk of sugarcane in her mouth. Locals often chewed on the perennial grass to extract the sweet juice, which most foreigners only saw or tasted in its white or brown refined state. Carmela gave Juanita a bear hug and then she knelt for the boys. They received a painful pinch on the cheek then suffocating hugs and kisses. Such was the custom of matriarchs in many cultures. Carmela lured the boys into her home by offering them some cane of their own from the kitchen. Juanita and Carmela walked back to the curb to retrieve the suitcase.

"Niña, what's going on in our country?" Carmela said. "Seeing you here with only one bag means that what I've been hearing in the streets is true. Castro's winning this war and will soon have control of the entire island. Many of us worry things will get worse if he takes over, as if that's even possible. His spies whore themselves for his favor. We can't trust anyone. I'm sorry, niña, I'm alone a lot and talk too much. Tell me about your husband and America."

Juanita tried not to lose her composure as she explained what transpired over the last several weeks. After hearing of Rigo and then America going after him, Carmela held her hand over her mouth and widened her already large brown eyes.

"No, Dios mio. I'm so sorry, my dear. You're welcome to stay as long as you need."

The ladies entered the house and headed to the kitchen where the boys were enjoying their third piece of sugarcane while chasing each other around. Carmela's home didn't have most of the luxury items found in America's house. She did have a television, and a large Motorola radio in the kitchen tuned to the Circuito Nacional Cubano station. The radio was introduced in 1922 and, as with the railroad, Cuba was the first Latin American country to have this technology. As they walked in, the radio jockey explained how the United States was in full support of the democratic process enjoyed by Cuba and its citizens.

"The United States will always be our friend and guardian if needed," the announcer said. "Democracy will be the only accepted form of government in Cuba and soon all Latin America. We will soon have this rebel insurrection put down and our true leader, El Presidente Fulgencio Batista y Zaldívar, will continue to move our country in the direction of freedom and prosperity for all who call Cuba home."

"Mi hijos, please go out back and play." Juanita said. "But don't chase the chickens. And please don't go into the sugar fields as I may not find you for weeks."

Carmela took Juanita's hand. "Juanita, you and the boys can take the extra room where I used to make my husband sleep when he snored." They both enjoyed a brief smile in the midst of the surrounding chaos. Carmela helped Juanita drag the suitcase into the room and then sat on the edge of the bed.

"I am scared for them," Juanita said. "How do I survive and raise my children in this country that I love so much? We must find a way out to the United States."

Carmela looked up to the ceiling. "God only knows what will happen to all of us. I also want to go to the United States, but I'm old, it's too late for me to create a new life in a place so different from ours. A man we trust in Varadero on the tip of the peninsula west of Havana has been making small boats for families that want to leave the island but can't get out now and may never if Castro takes over. Many take the hundred-mile trip to the States. Some use the Gulf Stream and get to Key West or other islands that are in the US. There's only a short window to take such a trip and I know some have left in the last few weeks. Maybe there's still time. He charges four thousand pesos for a small boat with supplies and instructions. I need to show you something."

Juanita slowly absorbed as much of this information as she could. It was too much to process all at once. It was overwhelming.

Carmela opened the closet door and lifted a small rug from the floor. A piece of wood appeared to be a missing from one of the four-inch planks. Carmela placed her finger in the grove and pulled up. A trapdoor revealed an exit to the ground beneath the house. "If anything bad happens, you should take the boys down the trapdoor and hide in the field." She closed the trapdoor and pushed two planks on the left side of the closet. They were hinged and moved to reveal storage space.

"Rebels come into my home looking for food and volunteers, sometimes twice a week. Some of my own family members have joined them. It makes me mad, but because of this, they don't harm me. I'll keep you and the boys safe if I can, but if you ever need to leave unnoticed, this is how. Keep your suitcase here, and if you need to escape, push it into the hiding spot then get your family out of the house. If they find your personal things, it won't matter who my family supports."

"Gracias, mi amiga." Juanita took Carmela's hand. "I cannot begin to tell you what this means to my children and me."

The small room had two single beds. Carlos and Francisco were quick to fall asleep in one of them. Juanita stayed awake the entire night thinking about possible situations where everyone would be safe and the family reunited. The more she thought about it the more she was convinced that going to the United States was the only way.

When America discussed this with her when they were planning a strategy, they had talked about using the money she was saving to charter a plane. There was never any talk about a boat or the Gulf Stream. She didn't really know what to think of this, but it seemed possible. How wonderful would it be to reach the shores of the United States with the possibility of raising her children in a country that was truly free? A country where if you worked hard you could accomplish or be anything you wanted. She played out this scenario many times over in her head. The route seemed dangerous but not as dangerous as staying in a country that wanted her family dead or imprisoned. Only thoughts of Rigo and his current situation interrupted the various scenarios and possibilities.

The rising sun, accompanied by noises of vehicles headed towards the farm, ended her cycle of reflection.

CHAPTER TWENTY

Survival at All Risks

"We shall draw from the heart of suffering itself the means of inspiration and survival."

-Winston Churchill

The boys were still curled up sound asleep. Juanita looked at her watch and squinted. It was 6:30 in the morning and the sun had just crested the tall stalks of cane. The workers would not be coming by automobile. She looked out the window. It appeared to be more than one vehicle—yes, clearly two.

She woke the boys and told them not speak a single word until she said they could. Carlos started to ask why and she quickly silenced him with a look. The boys could dress themselves but shoes were still difficult for Carlos. She told Francisco to help his brother and quickly shoved their pajamas in the suitcase and clicked the latches shut. Francisco helped her push the suitcase into the hiding spot.

She quickly made the kids' bed and straightened her own. All three went into the closet and shut the door as two military jeeps pulled up in front of the old farmhouse.

Carmela woke up to the noise of the engines and put on her robe. She stuck her head in the spare room, saw no one, and was sure Juanita had left already.

The visitors didn't knock but simply walked into her home. Most people in Las Ovas and other small towns in Cuba never locked their doors. This was beginning to change as several homes had been robbed since the start of the revolution. Carmela turned the corner to face four men in her kitchen.

One of them had his head inside the ice chest. He removed his head and a leftover chicken leg. "Hola, tia. Viva la Revolucion! Compadres, this is my Aunt Carmela I told you about. She doesn't yet see that we're making history but has been kind to our cause."

Humberto Perez was twenty-two years old and had committed to the revolution from the beginning. He was tasked with recruiting new soldiers and gathering supplies. He stayed primarily between Havana and Pinal Del Rio scouting for Castro and his rebel leaders. Humberto would often brag he had actually met most of the major revolutionary comandantes such as Che Guevara, Raul and Fidel Castro, and even William Alexander Morgan, El Americano, whom he considered a friend and leader of his revolutionary unit, the Second National Front of the Escambray. He told his aunt and anyone who would listen that there was a trusted American leading a column of over 125 men in Cuba. This was proof that even the USA was supporting Castro. He boasted of his loyalty to the yanqui who would help them get rid of the pig Batista.

"This house is for family, eating good food, and short stories, Humberto, not a sermon. So let's eat and leave the politics in the streets of Havana," Carmela would say when he went on and on. They sat in the kitchen for what seemed like hours. Carmela went to the back yard to gather fresh eggs from her chicken coop and cooked the rebel soldiers a breakfast of fried eggs, warm Cuban bread with butter, and café con leche.

From the closet, Juanita heard the men enter the house. The male voice was clear, "Viva la Revolucion!" They would kill her for sure, but what would they do first? Oh God! And with the boys there watching. She would wait for the right moment to slip out the trapdoor, which she had lifted before the men entered the house. She held her hands over the boys' mouths.

"All right, muchachos," Carmela said in what seemed a much louder voice, "I'll go get some eggs for you. Humberto, be a good boy and pour your friends some fresh milk."

At the moment Juanita heard the creaking noise of the door, she grabbed Carlos and lowered him through the trapdoor until his feet dangled just inches away from the ground. Then Francisco. She looked down at them and placed a finger against her lips, then sat on the edge of the hole and slid out onto the light grassy area beneath the house. Carlos could easily walk standing up but both Francisco and Juanita had to hunch over as they headed toward the field. Just briefly before entering the sugarcane maze, she caught Carmela's gaze from in front of the henhouse. They entered the field holding hands, and she prayed none of the guests had noticed.

It was difficult to navigate the cane fields, especially for Carlos. Juanita picked him up and carried him on her right hip as she had done so many times before. She wanted to make sure they were far enough away before they stopped. They walked at least seventy-five yards into the cane field before they stopped and sat down in a damp but mostly cleared area.

"We have to stay here for a little while," she whispered. "There are some people in the house that may not want us here. We need to be very quiet. Do you both understand me?" Looking scared, the boys nodded. She knew they would be hungry as well and reached behind her and found an almost ripe cane. She had no way to break the tuberous grass off or even into pieces. She turned to her boys and simply modeled how to chew on the cane. What a sight, the three of them eating from one stalk of sugarcane. They looked like flute players sharing one very large flute. Juanita asked the boys what they wanted to be when they grew up. "But you must whisper the answer."

"I want to be a famous actor," Carlos said, "and be on the television and have lots of cars and girlfriends."

"You're going to be the best actor in the world, Carlito. Just remember it's acting, and don't believe you're something you're not. Whether you're a famous actor or a man who works the fields, always be respectful of others." Carlos frowned as if puzzled.

"I want to be a soldier like dad," Francisco said maybe a little too loudly. "I want to have a big gun and shoot the bad guys that keep us away from our home. I would go into that house right now and make all of them go away and leave us alone. I would get rid of all the bad people, like Dad's trying to do."

Juanita didn't respond right away. A five-year-olds vocabulary didn't always line up with what was in his heart and mind. "You'll make a great soldier. I know you're brave and would do whatever was needed to protect the people you love. Sometimes people who hurt you are also hurt and don't understand the consequences of their actions. Sometimes they wish they could have made different decisions so no one got hurt. But it's impossible to change the past. So make sure you do your best to make good choices and try to use your head before your strength or a weapon."

Past 1:00 in the afternoon, Juanita decided she must go back to see if it was safe for them. After the boys woke up from a nap, she told them, "I'm going to leave you here for just a little bit to see if we can go back to the farmhouse and be safe from the men who don't want us there. Maybe even get some food. I need you both to stay here and wait for me. Is that clear to you both?" They nodded. "I'll be back as soon as I can. Don't make any noise and don't call me. If I don't come back before the sun goes down, I need you both to do something for me. Go to the house at the end of this road, tell the people you can't find me, and tell them who your father is. Ask them nicely if they can take you to the military base in Havana. They will then be able to bring us all back together. Now, repeat what I just said. Francisco, you first please."

The boys tried to repeat her instructions, and it took them several attempts before they had the plan down. Juanita kissed and hugged them both and headed for the farmhouse. The boys, holding hands tightly, stared at her.

Carmela had already fed her nephew and his rebel friends, yet they simply wouldn't leave. Humberto started to poke around the house. He left the kitchen and examined each room. He got to the spare room and paused to study the two beds.

"Muchacho, why do inspect my rooms?" She put on an air of authority she didn't feel. "Do the revolutionary leaders teach you to be nosy with your family?" Humberto simply studied the two beds and rubbed his chin. He walked to the closet and opened the door. Carmela fought down panic. He knew she'd been hiding something from him.

"Tia, we're going to need to stay the night here. We have a meeting in the morning in Pinal Del Rio. We also have some things we need to store here, but we'll be back for them after our meeting. This closet should be big enough for several of the Thompson machineguns the Cuban army just donated to our cause." He laughed then returned to the kitchen and asked the three soldiers to unload the machineguns from the jeeps and place them in the spare room closet.

Carmela could not refuse her nephew. She simply shook her head and threw a hand up in the air as if brushing off a fly. After a few more of his kitchen-table stories, Carmela excused herself, it was now 1:00 in the afternoon. "I need to take my afternoon nap. And I need some peace and quiet for a while." She was on her way to her room. "Try to whisper your stories of revolution and victory."

She was in her bedroom and about to close the door when Humberto called to her. "Tia, we want to take a little bit of your cane with us for our friends tomorrow. I keep telling them how sweet it is on your farm. I'll go out with the boys and cut some down, yes?"

She returned to the kitchen. "Humberto, why do you always brag about everything? Bien, if you want to take the best cane, cut it from the west side of the field. It's sweeter there and some of it's ready to be harvested." Carmela pointed away from where she'd seen Juanita and the boys enter the field. "The machetes are in the shed. Be sure to clean them off after you use them."

The four men headed out to the shed, and Carmela raced to her room. She locked the door behind her, pulled a yellow envelope and pad of paper from the bottom drawer of her dresser, and hurriedly drafted a letter, which she placed in the envelope before returning to the kitchen. She took a chunk of bread and some cured ham from the back of the ice chest, filled an empty milk bottle with water, then pulled out a used potato sack from underneath the sink. She looked out the window several times to make sure the men were still in the field.

Carmela placed all the items and the envelope in the sack and tied it closed with a loose knot. She could hear the men returning to the house. She ran from the kitchen to the spare room closet and opened the trapdoor. At the same time she heard the familiar creaking of the kitchen door, she dropped the sack onto the ground. She waited for the creaking to resume as the door was being closed, and lowered the door simultaneously.

"Humberto, I need to get my things out of this closet if you're going to store those God awful guns in here. Come, give this old lady a hand." Carmela desperately tried to still her racing breath and heartbeat.

Juanita reached the edge of the sugarcane and waited to see if the men had left. She carefully poked her head out from behind the stalks and saw two Cuban army jeeps. They did not however bear the familiar markings of the Cuban government but had "M-26-7" spray-painted on the doors, indicating that the vehicles now belonged to the 26th of July Movement, Fidel Castro and his rebels. She heard something. There was someone to her left coming out of the field.

She quickly took several slow and quiet steps backwards. She could see them, all four men. They must have seen her. Juanita held her breath and waited for them to reach her position. Another minute passed but no one showed up. Should she dare peek out again? She must find out if they spotted her. She slowly went to her knees and made her way to the end of the front row of cane. She looked out between two tall stalks.

There they were! But not headed towards her. As they entered Carmela's, something fell from the house—no, was dropped from the trapdoor.

The boys had been holding hands for over an hour without uttering one word to each other. Their palms were sweaty and sticky from the sugarcane. Carlos leaned over to his brother. "I love you, Francisco. I'm sorry I'm so much trouble. I want you to know in case something bad happens."

"Stop talking or someone will hear us. Nothing bad is going to happen. Mima will be back very soon. And...I love you too."

Juanita continued to watch the men in the kitchen from the edge of the field. She couldn't hear their voices, but their hand gestures told her they were engaged in a conversation. This was a long time for the boys to be alone, but she needed to see if the men would leave. The bundle dropped from the house must have been Carmela's, a signal or something intended for her. The timing had to be right. She had to wait for them to leave or go out to their jeeps. The vehicles were far enough away from the house that she might have enough time to reach the trapdoor opening area and retrieve what was dropped. Twenty more minutes passed.

The men left the kitchen and headed towards the front door. When she saw them reach the jeep, she dashed out of the stalks and ran. She was not an athlete, but she ran so fast she was sure one of her shoes would come off. She didn't even look at the men. She reached the old potato sack in less than ten seconds and took fifteen seconds to make it back. Breathing hard, she paused just inside the cane and peeked out again. They were carrying some things in through the front door.

She could see the boys before they could see her. They were shaking, their hands still locked together. Their free arms were wrapped around each other's neck and shoulders. They had clearly heard her approach and had braced themselves to see whatever hideous beast was coming for them. As she stepped into the clearing, the boys both released their death grip on one another and lunged towards her, each hugging one of her legs.

The three of them sat down and opened the potato sack. Juanita pulled out the water, which was a bit warm but still would help delay dehydration. She handed it to the boys and instructed them to take small sips and share. Next were the ham and the bread. They were so hungry that the few morsels seemed like a feast. Juanita reached back into the sack and retrieved a yellow envelope. She opened it and found a stack of money. "We're rich!" Francisco said. Juanita then counted the money, 5000 pesos. Finally, she held the letter. The last thing Juanita wanted was to read another letter telling her something had gone wrong. She unfolded it.

"*Juanita, I have left you this money in case you decide to leave the island. You have enough to get you to Varadero and pay for a boat. These men are rebels and will be spending the night. It is not safe here for you and the boys now. I will take care of your belongings. Write to me and let me know how to get them to you once you're settled. If you travel north to the end of the field, you will find a road. Head west for less than a quarter mile. There you can find a taxi in the village square. If decide on the course of action we spoke of earlier, please see our family friend. He can help you. His name is Alvaro Delgado and he can be trusted. Please take care of yourself and those two wonderful children. Con amor, Carmela.*"

The address in Varadero was written on the back of the letter. All she could do was hold the letter close to her chest, look up into the sky, and pray. The poor woman, whom she'd doubted at first, was a true friend. She had risked so much to help her and the children. She hoped one day she could repay the favor and at least return the money.

"All right, my strong big boys. We're going to walk off some of this food. Let's take a stroll in the field. I think we should head north."

CHAPTER TWENTY-ONE

Hope and Libertad

The walk in the field helped clear her mind. Although the farm was small in comparison to others on the island, it still took over thirty-five minutes to make it across the field, especially with two little ones in tow, who were again getting thirsty and hungry. The road was exactly where Carmela had explained. They made it to the village and found a taxi. All three of them sweating and looking ragged from being in the dusty field all day, entered the light-blue Chevrolet sedan with nothing except a potato sack and an envelope full of money.

Juanita told the taxi driver where they needed to go. He turned towards them. "That's a long drive. It'll cost two hundred pesos one-way. I'll need this paid before we leave." Juanita reached into the potato sack and produced the fare.

After driving awhile, he asked Juanita why she was going to Varadero. She made up a story about helping a relative clear an area of a sugarcane field. That was why they looked so unkempt. She had not bathed or changed clothes in two days. Her boys smelled of iron and copper when they sweated. She hoped it would mask her own odor. The driver asked her more questions. She attempted to change the subject, but it didn't work. She started talking to the boys as if she hadn't heard some of the questions. Like which farm they came from. Varadero was a well-known resort area developed by foreign interest. Many Cubans believed American mobsters were involved.

The driver put on a radio station playing older Cuban folk songs. Juanita recognized the tune immediately. It was "Siempre en mi Corazon" by Ernesto Lecuona, a popular pianist, who had been nominated in 1942 for an Oscar but lost to a song called "White Christmas" by Irving Berlin. She drifted off.

Their driver kindly woke them up a few minutes before reaching Varadero. The three of them had slept for almost four hours. The driver asked her where he should take them. Juanita had never been to Varadero and was taken by how pretty it looked. There were old colonial buildings in the Town Square, expansive new resorts, high-rise hotels covering most of the shoreline on the peninsula, and new mansions built for the wealthy and elite, mostly foreigners. How pathetic she and the boys must look wearing dirty clothes with only a potato sack as an accessory. Juanita reached into the bag, took out the letter and 20 pesos, and handed the bills to the driver. The address on the back of the letter was Carretera Las Morlas km 17,5 Sector Punta Hicacos Varadero. She looked at the boys and then back inside the envelope. She did not yet want to go meet the man Carmela spoke of.

"Can you please find us a small hotel on Carretera Las Morlas towards the northern tip of Varadero? I think it's time my boys ate some good food and cleaned up properly." The two children heard this wonderful news and began to smile and writhe in the back seat of the taxi. Juanita laughed. "On second thought, we'll go to the Varadero International Hotel."

They arrived just before nightfall and were surprised at the splendor of the new hotel. It was opulent even in comparison to the International Hotel in Havana. Juanita had never stayed at the Havana hotel but had gone to the Compay Segundo Hall in the lobby a few times with Rigo early in their relationship. She would dance with him and soak up the club ambiance. Rigo, however, was always on edge when they went out, especially at the Hotel International Havana. Juanita didn't know what to make of it and he never wanted to talk about it. God, how she missed her husband. She couldn't stop the tears from flowing down her cheek. She tried to compose herself before going in to find a room.

The doorman stared at them the entire time he held the door open and scowled while they approached the front desk. She was overcome with guilt at staying at such a place. They looked like peasants who just put in a long day cutting sugarcane in the field—which was indeed her background. She had grown up working the fields. She'd often looked exactly as she did at that moment, minus the tears.

The front desk took her seriously only when she produced the required pesos. They headed to the room, stopping at the gift shop to pick up some clothes and snacks. As they entered the room the kids took off exploring every nook and telling each other how great it was that they were staying in such a place.

After getting cleaned up and ordering room service, she finally felt human, and her strength started returning. Sleep would have been an added pleasure but did not present itself during the night. She couldn't stop her mind from racing. The boys slept soundly, as usual.

At 7:00 in the morning Juanita was sitting on the hotel bed staring at her two precious little boys, wondering what their fate would be. She would have to live with the decisions of the next few days for the rest of her life. After waking up the boys and dressing them in their new clothes, she called the front desk to request a taxi. As she hung up she thought of America. What was she going through? Was she even alive? She knew it would be a futile attempt but picked up the phone again and quickly connected to an operator. "F-2202 Pinal Del Rio, por favor."

America was an absolute disaster and looked like death had almost conquered her. Which it nearly did. She had hugged Berto so hard in thanking him that she may have caused additional damage where his arm used to be. He did not seem to mind. He simply walked away towards his shack, looking back at her and Jose several times. She then asked Jose to take her back to the Pinal Del Rio farmhouse.

She didn't have a plan yet but knew she needed to gather some belongings and leave the farm before it was too late. She didn't want to delay her departure and receive any unwelcome late-night visitors. Jose pulled into the dirt driveway of her farm, stepped out to open her door, and spoke his first words since leaving the airfield.

"Never in my life did I expect to be a part of something like this. I still don't believe this has happened. America, you have more courage than any woman, no, any person I know. God has been good to you this evening. May he keep blessing you and your family! I must leave now. None of us can be near this farm as it will surly become a dangerous place." He reached out to shake her hand.

America pushed his hand aside and lunged towards the fragile man. She embraced him for over a minute and they both shed several tears. She had known him to be a true friend for many years. If not for him, Rigo would still be a prisoner or dead. They both understood that this would likely be the last time they saw each other.

America broke the embrace. "Gracias, mi amigo. Your support and courage was beyond anything I could have expected, even from you, old friend. I will pray for you and your family to find peace on this island." As

Jose's car pulled out of the driveway, she turned to watch him leave the farmhouse for the last time. There would no doubt be more last goodbyes.

The phone in the kitchen rang. She almost tripped on a rug as she raced in hopes of hearing news from Rigo.

Juanita let the phone ring at least ten times. As she was placing the receiver down, she heard a voice on the other end. "Hola?"

"America, Dios mio, it's you! How are you, what happened in the last few days?" She was scared of the response she might get.

"Mi hija, we don't have much time and I'll make this brief. Rigo by this time should have landed in Montego Bay. He will be trying to make it to the United States and Miami soon."

Juanita slumped onto the floor. The children ran to her side. This time however, the tears were of joy, happiness and, more importantly, of renewed hope. "America, you're an angel sent from God." Juanita relayed the events of the last days.

America told her she would head to the second house they spoke of in the plan and then try to figure out a way to leave the island. Juanita asked her to come to Varadero and leave with them. America didn't want her to make her wait or be a burden to them.

There was a knock on the hotel door. Juanita panicked for a moment

"Señora, your taxi is waiting," the bellhop said.

"Juanita, you're a strong woman," America said. "I pray one day we can spend more time together and I can treat you all as you sincerely deserve."

The women said their farewells, and Juanita held the phone close to the two boys, who had been trying to listen to the conversation. They screamed their final goodbyes to their grandmother.

They reached the address on the back of the letter and stepped out of the taxi. Juanita had on a pair of American jeans that she bought in the hotel. The pants had four good pockets to distribute the money among so it wouldn't be too noticeable. She knocked on the door and prepared to talk to Alvaro Delgado. An older woman answered the door and greeted the three of them. Juanita smiled. "Hola, como estas? I'm Juana Gonzalez. I'd like to speak to Alvaro Delgado."

The older woman studied Juanita and the boys for several seconds. "I'm sorry, but there's no such man in this house. Goodbye." The older woman began to shut the door.

Juanita's heart sank again. Before the door completely closed, she yelled out, "Wait, please! I'm a friend of Carmela Perez. She sent me here to meet with Alvaro Delgado. She said he could be trusted and would help my children and me. Please señora, I understand you don't know me. We've been through so much and have come all this way for help."

The woman held the door only slightly cracked but appeared to be listening. She didn't reopen the door nor close it after Juanita finished speaking. After a minute, she uttered five words. "The back of the house." Then she closed the door.

Juanita tucked her new blouse evenly into her jeans and walked to the back of the old beach house. This one was built on stilts like Carmela's. The beach house, however, looked more worn and had not been well maintained. But it backed up to the water, and the views were amazing. The condition of the house could not take away from the natural beauty of the ocean.

The old woman walked out the back door and took a seat in a faded blue rocking chair on the rear porch. She pointed to a bench, and the three sat together tightly. She didn't say anything but pulled out an old cane pipe from a wicker table next to the rocking chair, took out a pouch of tobacco, and stuffed a wad into the pipe chamber. She scraped a large wood matchstick across the flint of the matchbox, lit the pipe, and took a deep draw. The entire process was carried out as if in deliberate slow motion.

"So, you say you know Carmela? What is this help you need from Alvaro?"

Juanita explained her situation to the old woman—Rigo being captured and America saving him from a firing squad. The woman smoked her pipe and looked out to the sea. She seemed to be nodding, but it could have simply been the rocking chair. After Juanita finished her story she sat and waited for a response. The rocking continued, as did the smoking. Several minutes went by in awkward silence.

"I'm sorry for your situation," the woman said. "We're all going through many troubles these days. Not knowing whom to trust is tiring. My name is Libertad and the man you speak of is my husband. I'm sad to say he is indeed not here. Not for over two weeks now. He was called into a meeting with the government, if you choose to call it that. This isn't the first time someone disappears after meeting with the Batista men. I believe they knew he was doing the very thing you are asking for yourself. Government men have also been trying to get us to sell our home to what they call 'friends of the government and president.' We'd never sell this house and have explained this to them more than once. I'm still hopeful but must prepare myself for what may follow. So, my new friend, you see we both have problems. This island seems to be a fertile breeding ground for them."

Juanita shared some words of sympathy with the woman and said her goodbyes. "Let's go, children, we must try to find a way to your father."

As Juanita turned the corner, Libertad cleared her throat. "So, Señora Juanita Gonzalez, have you ever been on a boat?"

CHAPTER TWENTY-TWO

A Lesson on the Seas

Varadero was a located on the narrow Hicacos Peninsula on the outside part of the Bahia De Cardenas in northern Cuba. It overlooked the Straits of Florida. Key West was approximately one hundred miles northwest across the Straits from Varadero. The voyage to Florida was dangerous, especially for an untrained navigator. Weather conditions played a key role. Many people had lost their lives attempting the trip in small boats. It was truly a desperate attempt to risk the passage without experience, a proper boat, and equipment. It was difficult for many to understand why a person would undertake such a treacherous journey unless they had themselves lived under tyranny and oppression in fear of the government and without hope.

Juanita and the children stopped in their tracks and stared back at Libertad, who smiled at them. "Come back to the porch, we may still have some more to talk about." Juanita returned to the porch but was not asked to sit this time. Libertad got up from her rocking chair and tapped her pipe upside down on the side of the old house to remove the ashes. She left the pipe on the wicker table and walked over to the boys. "You two gentleman are looking very bright this morning. If you mother doesn't mind, there are several balls underneath the porch you're welcome to play with."

Juanita nodded, and Carlos and Francisco raced off under the porch.

Libertad scanned the horizon and open waters. "I've known Carmela for many years. She's a good woman, you're lucky to have her as a friend. I've also met your mother-in-law, America. I imagine she can be what you would call 'difficult' at times." Juanita laughed. Libertad turned to face Juanita. "Are you sure this is what you want to do? I understand what you may be subjected to if you stay in Cuba but want to make sure this is a choice you have thought through."

Juanita stared out at the ocean and, for what might have been the first time, began to grasp the expanse of the waters surrounding her homeland. She knew nothing about the sea or navigating in such conditions. She had only rowed a few times with Rigo on a lake by the farm. It was indeed a great risk and could end up being the last mistake of her life. Or the boys' lives. But she had nothing left in Cuba. America would no doubt find a way to the United States soon. With both of her parents' dead, in terms of support, she was truly alone. How would the army, government, and rebels react if they found out Rigo had left Cuba? Would they go after family members like they had done on many occasions?

She desperately desired to be back in her husband's arms. She yearned to see his eyes, feel his touch. She wanted her children to know their father.

"If there's a chance to escape Cuba, I must try. I understand the dangers and will accept our fate. We can't stay here." Juanita reached into her pockets and pulled out the money she had left, about 4500 pesos after the taxi to Varadera and the hotel. "Carmela gave us this so we could get off the island."

Libertad looked down at the money. "Put that away. I won't take money that belongs to my friends. If you make it to the States, it'll help you get settled." She shrugged. "This is crazy. But sometimes crazy is good. Or the only thing left."

Libertad led Juanita to the end of the small pier and pointed northwest across the expanse of the ocean. "I don't know much about the sea but have heard my husband explain it enough times. There's no way you can ever make it out of Varadero during daylight. You must leave after nightfall around seven when the Marine Patrol eats dinner and is never seen. Travel northwest for a full day and row the boat as long and hard as your body can stand. This is the only way you can catch the Gulf Stream and get close to the Florida Keys."

She frowned at Juanita. "Listen carefully now. If you don't row hard, you may still catch the current, but it'll take you around the peninsula of Florida and up the Eastern Seaboard, which will lead to disaster. Unless a commercial vessel sees you, the three of you will surely die at sea. The possibilities of being found in a small boat are almost non existent."

Juanita took a deep breath and nodded.

Libertad took a softer tone. "You also can't carry much food and water in a small boat. If there's a storm, you won't survive. Even large boats have been overturned. The good news here is that I check the forecast every day and they predict no storms for the next three days. Although this can change in several hours."

Libertad looked her up and down. "What you're wearing is pretty but not good. You must cover all your skin. The sun will burn and eat away at your flesh. I have some clothes that should fit you and the children. You must drink water frequently to stay alive. You may not be thirsty but must still drink regularly. Make sure the boys drink too. Watch them, or they may not drink enough to stay properly hydrated. I have enough food and water to last three days. Anything beyond five or six days, God forbid, will lead to a most horrible death by starvation or dehydration."

Libertad gazed out to sea again. "Finally, the current can be tricky. Many sailed off and were returned to the very spot they left. You must row hard for the first day. I cannot make this point strongly enough. I will try to remember what else Alvaro would tell people, but I am old. I will need to think more on this. Now, do you have any questions for me?"

"Thank you for explaining all this. I do have one question. Where's this boat?"

CHAPTER TWENTY-THREE

Calm Waters During Troubled Times

Libertad headed back toward the house but stopped at the other end of the pier where the coast met the ocean. The dock was about seven feet above water, and the coastline had eroded the area under the pier over the years. She stepped off the pier and down the slope, carefully avoiding the water, and pointed underneath the pier. Juanita followed and peered into the shadows. A small cave appeared directly below the first few wooden planks, invisible unless you were underneath the pier. The recess went back about ten feet towards the house. Juanita still couldn't see what Libertad was pointing to until she got closer. There it was! A boat moored to a pole sticking out of the water.

At first and second glance, Juanita couldn't help but think it wasn't a boat at all but a bathtub. She took her shoes off and waded towards the craft. She could still smell the paint and lacquer recently applied. Two oars were inside the boat. There was just enough room for her to sit in it while the boys lay down next to each other. Was it possible this small boat could take her and her children to the United States and Rigo?

She studied it as if she knew what to look for and was a certified inspector of such things. She returned to dry land and Libertad, who was watching the children kick the ball in back of the house. "They're truly a gift but grow up so quickly. I will pray for all of you. My husband made that boat and over thirty others with his own hands. This was the last one he built. I haven't been able to part with it. Several people knocked on my door, but I turned them all away. He also made sure each boat was seaworthy and doesn't take on water. I would often go with him to test the boats. He never mentioned it to anyone, but he didn't even know how to swim. I tried to show him several times, but that man would just sink like a rock." They laughed together for short moment and walked back to the house, arms interlocked.

"Thank you, Libertad. I'll pray for your safety and your husband's return."

They called back to the boys and told them to come inside. Carlito wanted to keep playing. He had mastered the gift of foot stomping that children seem to learn intuitively.

Señora Delgado led them to the kitchen. "Now I must fatten you up and prepare your supplies."

Francisco looked up at his mother. "Are we going someplace, Mima?"

"Remember how you said you wanted to be a soldier? I believe we'll try you out as a sailor first."

Libertad collected supplies from the pantry and her bedroom. "The compass will help you stay on course. The flashlight will be useful if you see a ship at night." She grabbed the handle of the next item. "This bucket is very important. Pooping and peeing are very difficult to do on a boat. Especially for little ones, who often end up wearing most of it.

The blankets will keep you warm at night, as the temperature will drop severely after the sun sets." Finally, she pointed to the last of the supplies on the table. "Food and water. You must ration this out. Be very careful you don't drink or eat too much at one time. Separate this into rations for three days. The beef and fish jerky may not be too appetizing but will keep you alive. These canvas lister bags used by the military are light and won't leak. You have three here—one a day for the three of you. The clothes are on my bed. Take the children in later and change. You must all be in the boat and prepared to push off before seven tonight."

It was starting to become a reality for Juanita and a sense of fear and apprehension set in. Her mind wandered with doubt. She redirected herself quickly and came back to a place where she could find strength. She replayed the image of holding hands with Rigo on a field of lush green grass and wild flowers as they playfully flirted and watched the children run around. This was her happy place.

Day One at Sea

The day had flown by so very quickly. Juanita and the children went into Libertad's bedroom around 6:00 to change. The children's clothing was loose, but that was good. Any items that were too tight wouldn't allow the skin to breath under the hot Caribbean sun. Libertad and Juanita made several trips to the boat barefoot and secured the supplies. The boat had six metal cleats they used to tie down the necessities in case of rough winds or a storm. By 6:45 all the preparations had been completed, and the four of them made their final trip to the boat hand in hand. Libertad was holding Francisco's hand as they went down the slope. She released it only when she needed to untie the mooring.

The night sky was clear and moon partially visible, providing a little light for the travelers. Juanita placed Carlos in the boat first. Then she helped Francisco, who slipped trying to climb in on his own. Libertad needed to help Juanita in as the boat was now in deeper water that came up to her waist. She hugged the young mother.

"Be safe, Juanita!"

With her final words she pushed them towards the open waters. Juanita already had the compass on her lap and both oars secured in the horseshoe style oarlocks. They waved goodbye, and she quickly began to row with the front of the boat lined up with the needle on the compass pointing northwest. She had practiced the rowing motion with Libertad in the house but was surprised at how much resistance the water created. She kept rowing. The first thirty minutes were so difficult that she began to doubt herself again. The shoreline became smaller and smaller, and she contemplated turning around. Then she looked at the boys, sound asleep on a blanket. The trip was all her doing. Turning back was not an option. She needed to find strength from somewhere and continue.

Libertad had told her to maintain a rhythm as she rowed. Thirty strokes per minute was a good target. She tried to maintain the exact stroke count. She looked at her watch for the tenth time, and they had been in the boat for over an hour. The coastline was still visible but only slightly. The lights of Varadero marked where the sea and shoreline united and became dimmer with every stroke.

Two hours into the journey, she started to tire. She pushed past the pain and stopped only to check the compass and time.

Three hours in, her pace had slowed, but she knew she had to continue to row. Despite constantly rotating her grip on the oars, her hands began to blister. She tore off a small piece of her blouse and wrapped it around each hand and kept rowing. Their lives depended largely on this first night of hard rowing, and Juanita did her best to catch the current Libertad spoke of.

After five hours, she could no longer see the shoreline. It was no longer possible to turn back. She continued to row. The pain did not stop her. The waves began to intensify and crashed against the boat, occasionally taking her off course.

After seven hours of rowing, she could no longer maintain even the slower pace she had set for herself. She would row for fifteen minutes and take a break. Then for ten minutes. Finally, a break was needed every five minutes. Blisters had formed on both hands. She could feel the wetness as some of them had burst and oozed sticky fluid. Nothing visible except the waves as moon and stars reflected light on the ocean around them.

After ten hours at sea, the skies lightened. Carlito and Francisco were still sound asleep. Juanita was completely drained. She had rowed most of the night and it had been much harder than she imagined. Now she needed to rest more than she rowed.

The boys woke up a little after eleven hours into the trip. They could sleep through a hurricane. Juanita hoped her theory would never be tested. Everyone ate and drank their ration of food and water. Juanita needed energy to continue rowing. She hoped after eating she could increase her pace. The sun was starting to turn the chilly morning air into a warm breeze. It would only get hotter as the day progressed.

By noon they all had red faces. The hats Libertad provided did little to shade them from the sun. Seventeen hours into the trip, Juanita could no longer feel her hands. The clear liquid escaped the multitude of blisters and had turned red with blood that covered not only her hands but also the oars. She ripped off more of her blouse and wrapped them around her hands so there was a layer between them and the wooden oars. Still, more blisters formed.

Around 3:00, after hours in the sun beating down on them, Juanita created a makeshift tent for the boys by propping up the blanket over the supplies. The boys however couldn't stay underneath the cover long as it became scorching hot inside.

Why hadn't Libertad given her any gloves? It had to be difficult remembering everything needed on a trip like this one. Libertad had rowed only a short distance with her husband and probably didn't even know of the need. Juanita pushed through the pain, considered putting her hands in the sea for some relief, but realized the salt water would sting and do more harm than good.

After they woke up from their afternoon nap, the children complained and asked her multiple times to turn around. She explained the best she could and tried to draw their attention away from the heat and seriousness of their situation. She would tell them stories she had heard from her mother as a child. She even tried singing old songs with them. All efforts ended with a complaint of some sort.

It was over twenty hours into the trip when she noticed it. The small amount of water at the bottom of the boat was increasing.

"No, not now! We're too far out to return and have a long way left." The hope she had on the onset of their trip was replaced by panic.

The boys were scared as well. "Mima! I'm all wet and my feet are getting wrinkly," Francisco said. There were over three inches in the boat surrounding the little five-year-old. Juanita stopped rowing and removed the supplies that were in the pooling water to access the situation. She couldn't row and drain the water at the same time. She grabbed the bucket they had already used several times and handed it to Francisco.

"All right, boys. You're now my little sailors. Sometimes sailors have to work on their boats. Today we'll work on ours. Scoop up the water and throw it outside the boat. This will be just like when you two play on the beach. It will be fun, but make sure you take turns."

The boys liked the idea of playing and needed something to take their minds off the heat. Francisco began, and two minutes into the game Carlos requested the bucket saying it was his turn and his brother wasn't playing fair. After an hour the water level had lowered enough for Juanita to see the source of the leak. It was between two of the planks on the hull. She looked around the boat for anything to help seal the leak.

Carlos asked for some water, and she handed him the canvas lister bag that was almost empty. He drank from the bag, and Juanita then handed it to Francisco, who also drank some water. Juanita finished the remaining water. She folded the bag at the crease on the bottom and reached for the knife she had been using to cut the jerky. She shoved the crease of the bag into the separated planks where the water had been entering the boat. She used the knife to push the material deeper into the crack until the wadded-up bag could be forced no deeper into the fissure. They all stared for several minutes to make sure it had sealed. The boys looked at each other in surprise. No more water was entering the boat.

The boys leapt to their feet and gave their mother a hug, which almost capsized the boat. Carlos called her his hero.

"You make a great sailor, Mom." For a brief moment it all seemed like a perfect day. Until she noticed the clouds forming in the horizon.

Day Two at Sea

The clouds had turned dark and ominous. The boys went back under the makeshift tent and tried to sleep. Juanita continued to row. Her hands no longer had individual blisters but were one solid mass of blood and hanging skin flaps. She tried pushing through the pain and attempting to row with her wrists, anything to increase their chances. Then the rain came. It was not the torrential downpour she feared but a light rain that served to cool them off after a day in the sweltering sun. She welcomed it. Juanita looked up to the clouds and tried to catch the raindrops with her mouth. The rain only lasted an hour. The clouds soon parted, revealing the sky and millions of stars. It was beautiful and mystical. The stars would flicker and touch the small waves, exposing their curves.

Juanita felt something slowly moving the boat. It wasn't noticeable at first, but they had clearly moved even though she wasn't rowing. She looked at the compass and they were not headed northwest any longer but instead north by northeast. She continued to look at the compass and wasn't sure at first but yes! They were moving on their own. Could this be the current? If so, was it enough? Had she rowed enough, or were they being propelled into the open waters of the Atlantic Ocean? She peeked in on the boys, sound asleep and dry from the rain. She rowed northwest again until her hands hurt too much. She leaned back in the boat, rested her head on a lister bag, and closed her eyes, just for a minute.

When she woke up, the sun was rising. It was 6:30. She jerked upright with the pain of the water touching her open wounds, rocking the boat. It took her several seconds to gather her bearings and realize where she was. She slept so soundly even the water covering the back of her head and neck didn't wake her. She looked around the boat for another leak, found none, then checked the seal on the previous leak. That also appeared to be holding. Not until she turned to the stern of the boat did she realize the water hadn't come from outside the boat but inside. The lister bag she'd slept on was completely empty.

"Dios Mio! What have I done?" There was only one bag of water left for the remainder of the journey.

Juanita panicked and frantically scooped the water up with the bucket they had used to drain seawater from inside of the boat, but it already mixed with the standing seawater at the bottom of the boat. They now only had three gallons of water to share. God forbid they stayed at sea for more than two more days. They wouldn't survive on the amount of water they had left. She hoped there was enough for at least the boys to stay alive. She would not drink any more.

There was enough jerky to share but only a little bit left for a third day if needed. She had not rationed it out well the first day, and they ate more than they should have. She decided to spread out the food and water over three different times of the day.

The sun was much hotter the second day. They were all past the red face stage and began to develop small blisters. Juanita could no longer use her hands. She tried to row a few times using her forearm and the bend at her elbow. It did not make much of a difference and caused too much pain to the side of her body and breast. Francisco took a turn rowing. The oars barely touched the water as he skimmed the ocean with the oars, and even this lasted less than ten minutes. Carlos had to try as well. He braved out three minutes of air rowing.

By noon it became so hot the boys took off their shirts and pants while they were under their tent. Juanita didn't notice for several minutes but the sun was beating down on them from the opening at the bow. She made them put their clothes back on. Francisco had his hand in the ocean and was attempting to splash water on his face and his brother's, to the admonishment of their mother. She tried to explain that the seawater made it worse for them. The boys started crying. Juanita could do nothing but console them. She tried to block the sun from them with her shadow but couldn't remain standing up in the boat for long.

The supplies had dwindled down to a few pieces of jerky. Juanita had many blisters and cracks on her lips from the sun. She could barely speak because it hurt her lips and throat. She brought the boys close to her and simply held them. The rocking waves comforted them. She tried to sing but was only able to get a few words out before her voice faded. Francisco sopped up water from the boat with the blanket and wrung it out into the sea to make the deck more habitable.

As soon as the sun went down, she allowed the children to remove their shirts. The damp blanket soothed their skin. Around seven, the three were curled up on the deck. Francisco was the first to ask the question she'd been thinking about even before they pushed off from Varadero.

"Mima, are we going to die out here in the ocean?"

She thought deeply before answering. She didn't ever intentionally lie to her children, but providing hope was her responsibility. She also felt so much guilt for placing them in this situation.

"Mi hijos, we're all going to die one day. I don't believe it will be on this journey. I believe you both have great things to accomplish. You'll one day have a family of your own and think back on this time. You'll need to choose how you reflect on this adventure. You can see it as a tragic time where we all suffered. Or you can look back and remember that even though it was difficult, we all made it. We pushed through the discomfort and sacrificed a lot to be with the people we love. You'll both have to make these types of decisions the rest of your lives. You'll have people who hurt and disappoint you. This too will be painful, but you must learn to look past the pain. These people are often hurt themselves and as long as you're good men and living a healthy and happy life, their words won't inflict long-term damage. Find your strength in the people who truly love you. Hold on to the moments and images of happy times with good friends and family. This will help you become strong in the most important area, the heart. I'll love you both forever. You two are the most wonderful and precious gifts I've ever been given."

She didn't know if her words resonated or were truly comprehended by the boys. She started to drift off and allowed her mind to imagine the boys as fathers with their own children to nurture. She prayed they passed these sentiments on to their own children. The boys were falling asleep as well, and she began to sing a popular Cuban lullaby. "Duermete, mi niño, duermete, mi amor, duermete, pedazo de mi corazón."

Day Three at Sea

The third day was clear, and the gentle tropical breeze allowed for a sound and well needed slumber. Juanita woke up twice during the night and checked on the children. Fatigue and dehydration were taking their toll. She had little energy and feared she might not last another day at sea. The last water bag was less than half full. It would only be enough for the two children for one more day. It was still dark at around 6:00 in the morning, and she let the children sleep a little longer. She placed her arm on the edge of the boat and rested her head on her shoulder and arm.

She thought about the sun. What an interesting star. So critical to human existence and a thing of great beauty. Many took hope from its light. Its very presence signaled the dawn of a new day and announced a rebirth on our planet. It let us know we were still alive, at least for the beginning of the new day. It also could be a destructive force. The closer you were, the hotter it became, until whatever substance was in its path either exploded or disintegrated to nothing. On earth, exposure to the direct sun could take a life in a single day. It was the second sort of sun that greeted her on their third day at sea.

Juanita rose from the edge of the boat as the sun resumed its assault on their bodies. The boys didn't wake up until around nine, and she was glad they slept in. Their first words were requests for food and water. She was careful to give them just enough to ease their own pain until the afternoon drink. The food would only be enough for a morning and afternoon meal. She cut the two remaining pieces of fish and beef jerky in half. She didn't cut any for herself and handed the first half of fish to the children, who devoured it in seconds, Francisco nearly gagging on it as he swallowed the one small piece. Juanita then gave them a piece of jerky, but this time they did not eat. Francisco quickly handed his back to his mother.

"Mima, I'm so full I can't eat anymore. Please take mine. It's real good, and you need your strength too."

Her eyes welled up with whatever moisture remained in her. She was both proud of him and sad he was in this position because of her decisions. Carlito also handed his food to his mother. Juanita knew they were right. She needed to eat in order to stay alive and protect them. The irony of the moment didn't escape her.

She nibbled a bit off each piece and returned them. "Thank you so much, my angels. I'm now completely full and couldn't possibly eat another morsel."

The boys took back the remaining bite of meat. Their act of kindness reminded her how special her children were. Even at such a young age they recognized placing someone else's needs in front of their own. It was also a source of pain. She knew the food and water would be gone by afternoon. There would be no more acts of kindness and only the pain of hunger. She had never really known this type of pain until now. She had been hungry before, but now that hunger seemed so minimal in comparison to what they were currently experiencing. Juanita hoped there was a limit to this pain. This proved not to be the case with hunger.

Few words were spoken during the day. They attempted several things to keep the sun from hitting them directly. All three would hold the blanket up over their heads. This wouldn't last long. Their tired bodies could not maintain the position for more than a few minutes. They tried lying face down to keep the sun from assaulting their faces, but this was too uncomfortable and the heat on their back and neck were equally painful. These attempts went on until they ate. Juanita tried to hold off until later in the afternoon. Around 3:00 she handed out the remaining food to the boys. This time she took a nibble of both types of jerky before handing their pieces to each of them.

Next came the water. She had to physically take it from Carlito, who would have gulped all of it without being able to control himself. Francisco drank next and was careful to leave some for his mother. She was about to hand it back to him but it was such a small amount that it wouldn't have made a difference. She carefully placed the bag over her head and tipped it back. For the first time in over a day the warm liquid touched her ravenous and blistered lips. The water was delicious! It was better than manna from the gods. She felt she could consume an ocean full of the life-giving substance. But it was gone in a second.

They were all still the rest of the day. At 5:30 the sun began its descent to the west and slowly fell over their left shoulders. The boys were not sleeping yet but had their eyes closed. She was alarmed at first and confirmed they were breathing every few minutes. Two hours later she saw them.

Day Four at Sea

She wasn't sure if she was hallucinating, rubbed her eyes with the back of her mutilated hands and refocused. There was something there. Actually, there were many. She saw fins in every direction. She prayed they were dolphins or a type of friendly fish. She soon realized her prayers would not be answered this time. These fish were predators. They had thrived in the waters of earth for over 350 million years. This was their territory, and they appeared to be claiming it.

First, a nudge. Testing how the boat reacted to an inconsequential encounter with a shark. The second one was more powerful. Juanita saw them everywhere. Small fins and larger ones. The boys had fallen asleep but she wrapped her arms around them. She lay flat on the deck in case the sharks had somehow seen her sitting in the boat. She held onto the children tightly with the limited amount of energy she had left. This might be the last time she spent with her children. She wanted to feel them and keep this last memory until her final breath. What a terrible way to die.

"I'm sorry, my children, I'm sorry." Juanita began to wail as the sharks continued to bump into the boat. It was a muffled cry as her voice now was almost completely absent. They splashed about as if taunting their next victims. The boys awoke as they heard and felt the sharks ramming the boat. They did not sit up to look at the creatures that encircled them. She could see how completely drained they both were and wondered for split second if this was not actually a better way for them to die. She did not want them to experience the slow and painful death that hunger delivered. Their reaction was not what she expected. They simply looked at their mother and touched her face. They were actually smiling at her. Their voices were raspy and their pace of speech slow.

"Mima, it will be okay." Francisco gently touched his mother's blistered cheeks. "We love you and everything will be fine. I know it for sure. Remember what you told us last night? We'll make you proud, Mima. We'll soon be back with Pipo."

"Do you think he'll remember me, Mima?" Carlito said. "I was a baby when he left. Maybe he doesn't remember me."

She could not speak and felt her body betray her as the physical and emotional trauma took control of the moment. She began to convulse as her children hugged her even harder. She didn't want to die like this in front of children, but it wasn't her decision. One more shark smashed into the boat right before she lost consciousness.

The subject of a Heaven has been widely debated. Is it a location or a concept? If you believe it's a location, then you may or may not have an opportunity to see it for yourself. This would rely on many variables depending on your faith and behaviors while here on earth. A location is described in the Bible, and some believe there will be pearly gates and a multitude of instruments making a sweet sound as you enter this realm. It's a comforting thought for those of faith and conviction. For others, Heaven is part of a concept of earthly existence. It could be found in a beautiful location or a moment shared between people, and no other words could capture the magic and bliss experienced.

The sea was tranquil as it greeted the rising sun, calm as glass. The orange-yellow glow of the sky deepened the blueness of the Atlantic Ocean. It was here the little boat rested. Francisco was the first to wake. He looked at his brother Carlos, who had his thumb in his mouth like he did as an infant. He reached over and shook his younger brother. His voice only produced odd sounds barely audible. Carlos was slow to acknowledge the nudging but eventually opened his eyes. They were still on the deck of the boat. They stared at each other as if asking, what do we do now? They looked over and saw Juanita facing away from them on the boat. Just above her was a missing section of the boat in the shape of a semicircle. As both boys crawled towards their mother they saw a tooth sticking out of the new curve.

They attempted to turn Juanita, but her body was too heavy. They both shook her and called out with their raspy voices.

The children continued for several minutes but she didn't wake up. The boys simply draped their bodies on her and rested.

Juanita was at peace dying. Her only concern was her children. She would have so loved to see her husband one more time. She made the decision, and now the price must be paid. It was a fool's errand to attempt to cross an ocean with no experience. How completely reckless of her. Her cold body was on the deck of a little boat.

There was something very familiar about her surroundings. She attempted to pull through the haze and fog of dehydration. She felt warmth. Was this the way we transition to Heaven or to Hell? She wasn't sure but the presence she felt began to weigh on her. She attempted to open her eyes but the sun was already too bright. She not only felt it now but also heard it. It was breathing. She had to open her eyes to see what it was. She squinted at first but could only make out the outlines. Were these angels? Yes, they were definitely angels. Both rested their full weight on her. As she opened her eyes wider they began to smile at her. This was indeed Heaven. This place with her two children could not be mistaken for another.

She opened her arms and hugged them. They embraced for several minutes. Her voice was completely gone. She gestured to them with both thumbs of her marred hands to help her up. It took the three of them to sit her up. The boat however did not rock in the usual manner. She squinted and tried to make out shapes on the horizon. The slight waves swayed the small boat to-and-fro but only gently. She rested her head where the shark had apparently tried to pull her into the water and during the process took a chunk of the boat with him. The boat was resting on a rock...with sand all around. She couldn't speak but mouthed the familiar Cuban phrase, "Aye, Dios mio!"

Her vision returned, and she saw the coast. There were several green and white buildings. It reminded her of the barracks on the military bases in Cuba. And there was a flag. She tried to make out the colors on the flag. The horrible thought just came to her. What if they had simply drifted back to Cuba? She could make out the blue and the red but how many stars? It was hard to determine if there was only one star. She rubbed her eyes several times trying to focus her vision. She now saw the stars. There was not just one star but many of them. Could this be true?

Three Coast Guards approached their small vessel. They were gentle with the three survivors, who didn't understand a word but it was a sweet sound. "You are now in United States territory and will be processed as political refugees."

Afterword

I am sharing this story from the perspective of a Cuban, an American, and a Cuban American. For whatever the words in this book meant to you, they were simply my reflections on life, an exploration of personal history in order to more fully comprehend my present.

When I was growing up, there were four Cubas—actually, five. Although the Cuba ruled by my mother was not official, I was afraid sometimes you could possibly die in that Cuba just as easily as the others.

The first Cuba was the child of American business, of American gangsters, a product of the domino theory espoused by American presidents. It was the Cuba dear to the heart of its American patrons. President Fulgencio Batista ruled from somewhere I had never seen. He and the loyalists had embraced the notion that the Americans would never allow their jewel of the Caribbean, their little brother 90 miles from Florida, to fall into the hands of the revolutionaries, so they continued with life as they knew it—squeezed money out of the people, extorted money out of the Americans, and ate lobster. Every once in a while there would be a panic caused by some news report that America, embroiled in more lucrative ventures or a public confrontation with the communists, would stop sending Batista money. Or the American mafia would relocate their casinos to Las Vegas, or the sugar farmers in America would gain the upper hand in congress and all the under-the-table bribes to American senators would no longer work, and then the bank accounts would be emptied and loyalists would board planes for Madrid, Rio, or Santo Domingo. But mostly they stayed, continued to deny the sentiments of the people, and ordered flan for dessert.

The Second Cuba was in the jungle. Doctor Ernesto "Che" Guevara de la Serna smoked Cuban cigars, but that didn't make him Cuban. To the Cuba in my mother's kitchen, and Batista's Cuba in the casinos, he was an opportunist, an intruder. He was a doctor of medicine, a member of the lobster and flan set that had turned his back on privilege and embraced communism. How could you respect someone like that? He did not see Cuba as the rest of us did. His vision of Cuba linked it with a Latin American Communist Confederacy, an LACC to link with the USSR. My mother and Batista did not take Che seriously. However, the Castro brothers and the third Cuba did.

Fidel Castro was the third Cuba, the son a sugar plantation owner, born into a family of wealth and status. He attended private boarding schools and studied law at the University of Havana. He was a talented student and had political ambitions and anticommunist leanings early in his life. He was planning on running for political office until General Batista overthrew the Cuban government in 1952 and declared himself president for life. If the general was president for life, it meant that Fidel wasn't. Fidel's political ambitions simmered and finally exploded in July of 1953 when he and 150 citizen soldiers tried to awaken the people to revolution by assaulting the Moncada Military Barracks. The people weren't ready. They hadn't been squeezed enough, they still had a little bit of money left over for rum and cigars after working the fields and enough freedom to say, "Oh, things aren't that bad." Fidel was captured, tried, found guilty, and sentenced to 15 years. But, like many things in

Cuba, appearances are not what they seem. Batista's attempt to gain favor with the working class prompted him to release Fidel in 1955. This mistake would haunt the President to his grave.

The fourth Cuba was the people, and their conviction to cast their lot with whoever might actually end their poverty, end the corruption, and stop the whoring of Havana to the highest bidder. They finally had been squeezed and imprisoned and robbed and beaten enough so most of them found new hope with the bearded revolutionaries in the jungle. Che looked like Fidel and Fidel looked like Raul and then there were only two Cubas—Revolutionary or Loyalist. By 1959, when Batista emptied the banks and fled to the Dominican Republic, my Cuba had begun the process of sailing for Miami.

The Cuba of the People produced me. My grandmother America Gomez Gonzalez was a descendant of Cuba's indigenous Taino Indians. Before Columbus there were the Taino, and then there were the Spanish for the next four hundred years. The only reason there were any full Tainos left was that the colonial government and the Roman Catholic Church forbade marriage between the superior and inferior races, between the civilized and the "savage." Of course the Church and government couldn't completely control sex and procreation, but when a child was born interracially, he was always a Taino, never a Spaniard. The Taino continued to exist as an endangered species.

America was born on the Fourth of July in the fields of sugarcane in Pinar Del Rio. She had an abusive and controlling father. When she was five, she started working the cane, and every day she heard her father say three things: the only escape from the cane would depend on marrying well, until then you had to have a strong back, and always an unbreakable heart. The eventual graduation exam, which tested these attributes, came in the shape of Enrique Gomez whose family owned a lucrative construction business and the sugarcane farm leased out to the United Fruit Company. America was seventeen, Enrique twenty-four. It was a beautiful spring day in Malecon de la Havana when they first met.

Thank you for letting me share some of my Cuba with you!

About the Author

Dr. Charles Anthony was born in Havana, Cuba and raised in Chicago, Illinois by his parents, Rigoberto and Juana Gonzalez. His grandmother America also immigrated to Chicago from Cuba and was an important part of his life as a young man. He has a bachelor's degree in political science from the University of Florida and holds a master's degree in secondary education from Grand Canyon University and a master's degree in educational leadership from Northern Arizona University. He also received a doctorate in educational leadership from Northern Arizona University. He is currently a clinical professor at Arizona State University.

Charles has served as a principal for an online middle school, blended learning center, and assistant principal for a high school. He has taught social studies at Arizona College Prep in the Chandler Unified School District holding a multitude of leadership responsibilities. Charles was previously employed with Wells Fargo Bank for 13 years and held executive positions as vice president with Wells Fargo Financial. He helped create and develop the Emerging Markets Group for the company. He left Wells Fargo to pursue a career in education and fulfill his goal of helping others find the very best in themselves.

Additionally, Charles served in the United States Army and Army Reserves for over 23 years as a Cavalry Scout, Communications officer, and Military Intelligence officer. He is a combat veteran and has served in Iraq, Kuwait, Korea, Egypt, and many other areas across the globe. He has completed six marathons, two triathlons, and the Grand Canyon Rim to Rim Trek. His passion is his family. He loves spending time and traveling with his wife Nikala and two adult children, Christian and Lauren.

Made in the USA
San Bernardino, CA
19 May 2019